W9-CXQ-282

BASIC GOALS IN SPELLING

fifth edition

William Kottmeyer & Audrey Claus

Webster Division, McGraw-Hill Book Company
New York St. Louis San Francisco Dallas Atlanta

William Kottmeyer has served in the St. Louis Public Schools as teacher, principal, reading specialist, and superintendent. A nationally recognized educational innovator, Dr. Kottmeyer has created a wide variety of basic language-skills materials. Currently author-in-residence in the Webster Division, his publications include *Basic Goals in Spelling,* the *+4 Reading Booster, Decoding and Meaning,* the *+10 Vocabulary Booster,* the *Classroom Reading Clinic, Dr. Spello,* and the *Everyreader Series.*

Audrey Claus has served in the St. Louis Public Schools as teacher, consultant, elementary principal, and curriculum coordinator. Presently author-in-residence in the Webster Division, Miss Claus is co-author of *Basic Goals in Spelling* and the *+10 Vocabulary Booster.*

Sponsoring Editor: Martha Alderson
Editing Supervisor: Mary Lewis Wang
Designer: Catherine Kimball Scar
Production Manager: Leo B. Painter

The illustrations in this book were created by Marilyn Lucey, Diane Paterson, and Kyuzo Tsugami. Handwriting models were supplied by Zaner-Bloser, Inc., and are compatible with the *Creative Growth with Handwriting* series.

Library of Congress Cataloging in Publication Data
Kottmeyer, William, date.
Basic goals in spelling.
SUMMARY: An eight-volume elementary spelling series. Units in each volume are organized around a speech sound or syllable pattern, demonstrating ways in which these can appear in American English words.
1. Spellers. [1. Spellers] I. Claus, Audrey, date. joint author. II. Title.
PE1145.2.K6 1976 428'.1 74-8842
ISBN 0-07-034307-1 (v. 7)

Table of Contents

Spelling Alphabet

The letters of the alphabet are written symbols which we use to spell words. There are twenty-six letters in our alphabet. Each letter of the alphabet has a capital and a lower-case form. The handwriting models below show the way to write the capital and lower-case forms of each letter.

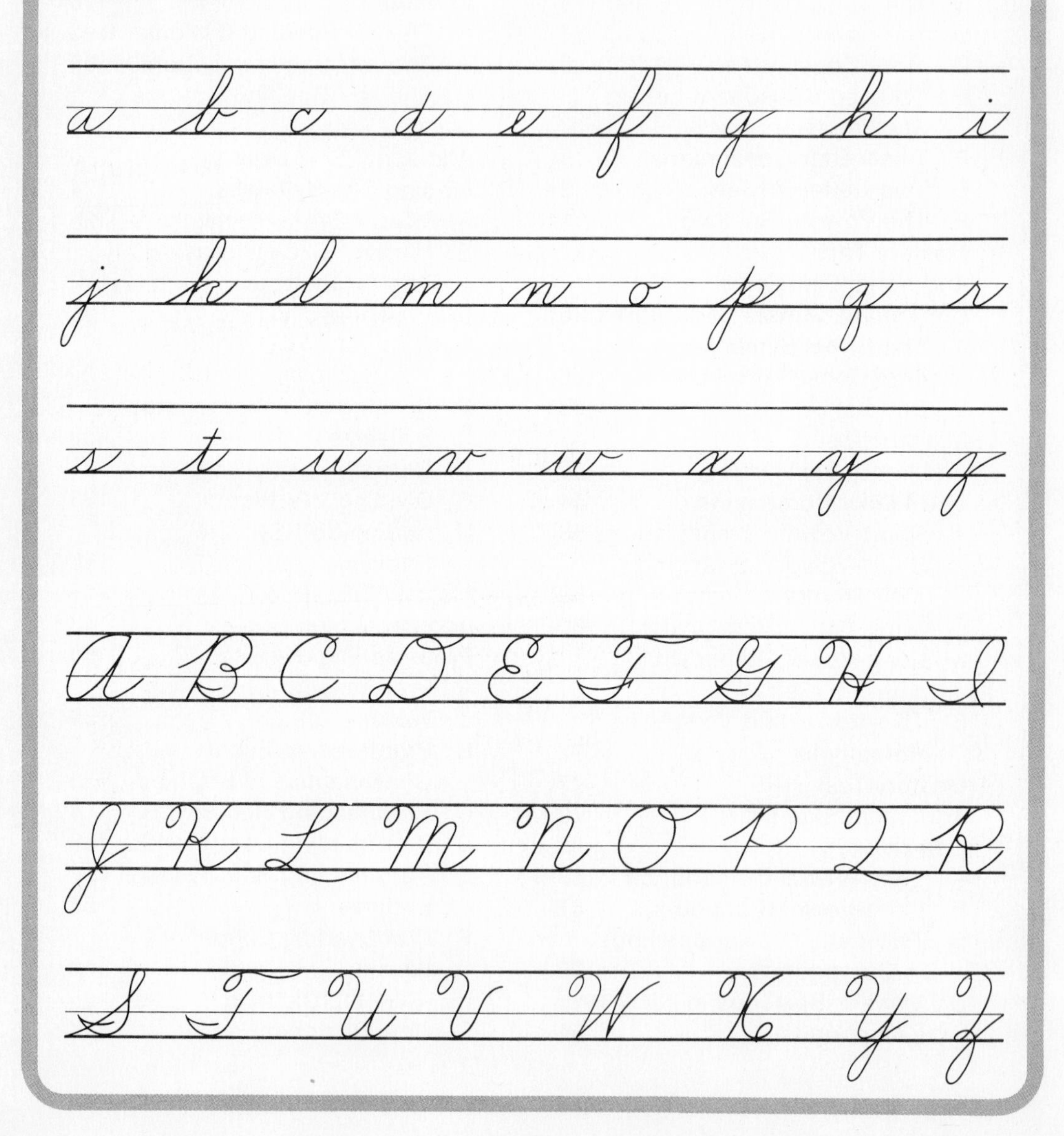

Sound-Spelling Alphabet

We show the pronunciation of a word by using special symbols inside slant marks. There are forty-four sound-spelling symbols, one for each of the dictionary sounds. A sound-spelling symbol always stands for the same sound, no matter how the sound is spelled in a word.

Consonant Symbols

/b/ big
/d/ did
/f/ fife
/g/ gag
/h/ hot
/j/ judge
/k/ kick
/l/ lull
/m/ mum

/n/ noon
/p/ pop
/r/ rare
/s/ sense
/t/ tot
/v/ valve
/w/ wet
/y/ yes
/z/ zoo

/ch/ church
/hw/ when
/ng/ sing
/sh/ ship
/ŧʜ/ this
/th/ thin
/zh/ vision

Vowel Symbols

/a/ ran
/ā/ rain
/ã/ care
/ä/ car

/e/ hen
/ē/ he
/ėr/ her

/i/ in
/ī/ ice

/o/ not
/ō/ no
/ô/ off

/u/ us
/ū/ use
/ü/ tool
/u̇/ took

/ou/ cow
/oi/ boy

/ə/ about
taken
pencil
lemon
circus

1 Sounds, Symbols, and Spellings

You can find the pronunciation or meaning of words in the dictionary. The dictionary lists *entry words* in alphabetical order. The *entry words* are spelled with the twenty-six letters of our alphabet. But the pronunciations of the entry words are shown in sound symbols. The dictionary must use one symbol—and only one—for a sound.

There are two kinds of sounds: consonant sounds and vowel sounds. To make vowel sounds, you let your breath come out freely. To make a consonant sound, you partly block your breath stream.

The Short Vowel Sounds and Symbols

Some of our vowel sounds are called the *short* vowel sounds. Use vowel spelling letters as sound symbols for these short vowel sounds.

/a/ is the vowel sound in

/e/ is the vowel sound in

/i/ is the vowel sound in

/o/ is the vowel sound in

/ô/ is the vowel sound in

/u/ is the vowel sound in

Consonant Symbols and Spellings

We use thirteen letters to represent the same sounds in dictionary sound-spelling as they do in regular spelling.

Consonant Sound Symbols	Beginning Sound of	Examples	Sound-Spellings
/b/		bed	/bed/
/d/		dog	/dôg/
/g/		gun	/gun/
/h/		hat	/hat/
/l/		lamp	/lamp/
/m/		man	/man/
/n/		net	/net/
/p/		pin	/pin/
/r/		rat	/rat/
/t/		top	/top/
/v/		van	/van/
/w/		web	/web/
/y/		yell	/yel/

Skill Drill 1 Write these short-vowel one-syllable nouns. Check your answers at the end of Chapter 1.

The Long Vowel Sounds and Spellings

Some of our vowel sounds are called the *long* vowel sounds. Use the short-vowel symbols with a line, a *macron,* above them for these long vowel sounds.

/ā/ is the vowel sound in

/ē/ is the vowel sound in

/ī/ is the vowel sound in

/ō/ is the vowel sound in

/ū/ and /ü/ are the vowel sounds in and

In regular spelling we can spell each of these long vowel sounds in several ways.

Sound Symbols	Spelling Options	Examples	Sound-Spellings	Your Examples
/ā/	ai	train	/trān/	1
	ay	tray	/trā/	2
	a-*consonant*-e	grape	/grāp/	3
/ē/	e	me	/mē/	4
	ee	heel	/hēl/	5
	ea	heal	/hēl/	6
	e-*consonant*-e	eve	/ēv/	7
/ī/	y	try	/trī/	8
	i(gh)	bright	/brīt/	9
	i(nd)	blind	/blīnd/	10
	ie	tie	/tī/	11
	i-*consonant*-e	mile	/mīl/	12
/ō/	o	go	/gō/	13
	o(ld)	hold	/hōld/	14
	oa	boat	/bōt/	15
	oe	toe	/tō/	16
	ow	tow	/tō/	17
	o-*consonant*-e	note	/nōt/	18
/ū/ *or* /ü/	ue	glue	/glü/	19
	ui	suit	/süt/	20
	ew	new	/nü/	21
	u-*consonant*-e	mule	/mūl/	22

Skill Drill 2 There are twenty-two long-vowel spelling options in the chart. Add your own example for each one. Copy each spelling option and then write your example beside it. For example, you might begin your list like this: 1 *ai,* grain. When you have finished, check your answers with the suggestions at the end of Chapter 1.

Skill Drill 3 Write a regular spelling for each sound-spelling. Use the chart to help you. Check your answers.

1 /brān/
2 /bēd/
3 /līt/
4 /trīb/
5 /grō/
6 /pōl/
7 /dün/
8 /rül/
9 /bōn/
10 /rā/
11 /hāt/
12 /dēd/
13 /prī/
14 /bīnd/
15 /hōld/
16 /wō/
17 /trü/
18 /tüb/
19 /brü/
20 /pī/
21 /gōl/

Skill Drill 4 Write a regular spelling for each of these sound-spellings. Use the charts. Check your answers.

1 /grān/
2 /mēn/
3 /drī/
4 /tīt/
5 /bōld/
6 /mōn/
7 /trü/
8 /drü/
9 /dā/
10 /grēn/
11 /pāv/
12 /grīnd/
13 /prīd/
14 /līd/
15 /blō/
16 /hōp/
17 /rüd/
18 /prün/
19 /tō/
20 /ām/
21 /drēm/

More Consonant Sound Symbols and Spellings

Besides the thirteen consonant letters listed in Section B, the dictionaries use five other consonant letters as sound symbols. In regular spelling, these consonant sounds can be spelled in several ways. In sound-spelling, use the same sound symbol, no matter what the regular spelling may be.

Consonant Sound Symbols	Spelling Options	Examples	Sound-Spellings	Your Examples
/f/	f	fine	/fīn/	1 ____
	ph	phone	/fōn/	2 ____
	gh	rough	/ruf/	3 ____

Consonant Sound Symbols	Spelling Options	Examples	Sound-Spellings	Your Examples
/j/	j	jail	/jāl/	4
	g (*before* e, i, *or* y)	gem	/jem/	5
	dge	edge	/ej/	6
/k/	c	cane	/kān/	7
	k	kite	/kīt/	8
	ck	kick	/kik/	9
	ch	ache	/āk/	10
/s/	s	sent	/sent/	11
	c (e, i, *or* y)	cent	/sent/	12
	sc (e, i, *or* y)	scent	/sent/	13
/z/	z	graze	/grāz/	14
	s	raise	/rāz/	15

Skill Drill 5 There are fifteen spelling options in the chart. Copy each spelling option and write beside it your own example of a word with that spelling. Check your answers.

Doubled Consonant Letters Spelling One Consonant Sound

Certain consonant letters are often doubled in our regular spellings. These two consonant letters spell one consonant sound, so the sound-spelling will use only one sound symbol for the two letters.

ebb /eb/	egg /eg/	err /er/
add /ad/	bell /bel/	pass /pas/
cuff /kuf/	inn /in/	mitt /mit/

Two-Letter Consonant Spellings and Their Sound Symbols

Because there are only twenty-six letters in our alphabet, two or more consonant letters sometimes are used to spell one consonant sound. Two-letter sound symbols also represent consonant sounds in sound-spelling.

Notice in the chart, for example, that the last sound in the word *sing* is spelled *ng.* The sound symbol for that sound is /ng/. The sound /ng/ might also be spelled with *n* before a *k* as in *pink* or with *n* before a *c* as in *zinc.*

Sound Symbols	Spelling Options	Examples	Sound-Spellings	Your Examples
/sh/	sh	ship	/ship/	1
	ch	chute	/shüt/	2
/ch/	ch	chop	/chop/	3
	tch	match	/mach/	4
/th/	th	thin	/thin/	5
/ᴛʜ/	th	them	/ᴛʜem/	6
/ng/	ng	sing	/sing/	7
	n(k)	sink	/singk/	8
	n(c)	zinc	/zingk/	9
/h/ /w/	wh	whale	/hwāl/	10
/k/ /w/	qu	quit	/kwit/	11
/k/ /s/	cks	tacks	/taks/	12
	x	box	/boks/	13

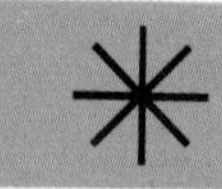

Skill Drill 6 There are thirteen spelling options in the chart. Copy each one and write your own example beside it.

Skill Drill 7 Write a regular spelling for each of these sound-spellings. Use the chart to help you spell the words. Check your answers.

1. /fōm/
2. /chōk/
3. /thangk/
4. /tasks/
5. /lach/
6. /kwāl/
7. /frāz/
8. /hūj/
9. /kāp/
10. /āk/
11. /hōz/
12. /krush/
13. /hwīt/
14. /fiks/
15. /skwint/
16. /jōk/
17. /baj/
18. /kāv/
19. /stik/
20. /pres/
21. /thril/
22. /kling/
23. /stiks/
24. /hwiz/
25. /spās/
26. /fās/
27. /jungk/
28. /ŦHem/

Skill Drill 8 Write a regular spelling for each of these sound-spellings. Check your answers.

1. /frīt/
2. /kis/
3. /chü/
4. /kwilt/
5. /neks/
6. /ruf/
7. /hej/
8. /skēm/
9. /sēnz/
10. /kwiz/
11. /shril/
12. /taks/
13. /ringk/
14. /ŦHēz/
15. /spēk/
16. /krīm/
17. /fāz/
18. /fus/
19. /shak/
20. /laf/
21. /rāj/
22. /skwēl/
23. /chōz/
24. /shef/
25. /skrach/
26. /thingk/
27. /hwīn/

Two-Letter Vowel Spellings and Their Sound Symbols

Because there are so few vowel letters in our alphabet, combinations of two letters are sometimes used to spell certain vowel sounds. A single sound symbol is used for each of three of these vowel sounds, and two sound symbols for the other two. The dictionary always uses the same sound symbol or sound symbols for sounds, no matter what the spellings may be.

Sound Symbols	Spelling Options	Examples	Sound-Spellings	Your Examples
/ü/	oo	moon	/mün/	1
	u-*consonant*-e	rule	/rül/	2
	ew	chew	/chü/	3
	ue	blue	/blü/	4
	ui	suit	/süt/	5
/u̇/	oo	book	/bu̇k/	6
/oi/	oy	boy	/boi/	7
	oi	oil	/oil/	8
/ou/	ou	mouth	/mouth/	9
	ow	down	/doun/	10
/ô/	aw	law	/lô/	11
	au	haul	/hôl/	12
	a(l)	hall	/hôl/	13

Skill Drill 9 There are thirteen spelling options in the chart. Copy each one. For each spelling option in the chart, write your own example of a word that uses the same spelling option for the same sound. Check your examples with the suggestions at the end of Chapter 1.

Skill Drill 10 Write the regular spellings for these sound-spellings of words that have two-letter vowel spellings. Use the chart to help you spell the words. Check your answers at the end of Chapter 1.

1 /fül/
2 /hôlt/
3 /hôk/
4 /swüp/
5 /boi/
6 /fôlt/
7 /koil/
8 /spout/
9 /skoul/
10 /lônch/
11 /yôn/
12 /bru̇k/

Skill Drill 11 Write the regular spellings for these sound-spellings. Check your answers.

1 /skül/	**5** /kül/	**9** /kroud/
2 /krůk/	**6** /kount/	**10** /hônt/
3 /skôld/	**7** /joi/	**11** /sprôl/
4 /klô/	**8** /point/	**12** /vôlt/

The Vowel-*r* Spellings and Sound Symbols

When the /r/ consonant sound follows a vowel sound, it usually changes the vowel sound. There are five vowel-*r* sound symbols. The vowel-*r* sounds have eleven common spellings.

Vowel-*r* Sound Symbols	Spelling Options	Examples	Sound-Spellings	Your Examples
/är/	ar	star	/stär/	1
/ãr/	are	care	/kãr/	2
	air	hair	/hãr/	3
/ôr/	or	for	/fôr/	4
	ore	more	/môr/	5
	oar	roar	/rôr/	6
/ėr/	er	her	/hėr/	7
	ir	sir	/sėr/	8
	ur	fur	/fėr/	9
/ir/	ear	dear	/dir/	10
	eer	cheer	/chir/	11

Skill Drill 12 There are eleven vowel-*r* spelling options in the chart. Copy each one and write your own example beside it. Check your answers.

Skill Drill 13 Write the regular spelling for each sound-spelling. Use the chart on page 11 to help you spell the words. Use the answer key at the end of Chapter 1 to check your answers.

1 /skôrch/	**6** /lãr/	**11** /rir/
2 /shãr/	**7** /kôr/	**12** /hwėrl/
3 /stir/	**8** /bôrd/	**13** /chėrn/
4 /bėrn/	**9** /vėrb/	**14** /skwãr/
5 /skärf/	**10** /skwėrm/	**15** /thėrd/

Skill Drill 14 Write the regular spelling for each sound-spelling. Use the chart on page 11 to help you spell the words. Use the answer key at the end of Chapter 1.

1 /skwėrt/	**6** /kėrb/	**11** /skãr/
2 /snir/	**7** /smir/	**12** /chôr/
3 /härsh/	**8** /jėrm/	**13** /chãr/
4 /spãr/	**9** /kôrs/	**14** /stôrz/
5 /spôrt/	**10** /snôr/	**15** /skôr/

Summary

This chapter has reviewed the consonant and vowel sounds and spellings that occur in one-syllable words. It has reviewed twenty-four consonant and eighteen vowel sound symbols and their regular, or expected, spellings.

The regular one-syllable vowel spellings fall into these four large groups:

1 short-vowel spellings
2 long-vowel spelling options
3 two-letter vowel spelling options
4 vowel-*r* spelling options

The charts on the following pages list the forty-two consonant and vowel sound symbols, show the spellings or spelling options for each one, and give examples in regular spellings and sound-spellings.

Spelling and Sound Symbol Chart for One-Syllable Words

Consonants

Consonant Sounds	Spellings	Examples	Sound-Spellings
/b/	b	bed	/bed/
	bb	ebb	/eb/
/d/	d	dog	/dôg/
	dd	add	/ad/
/g/	g	gun	/gun/
	gg	egg	/eg/
/h/	h	hat	/hat/
/l/	l	lamp	/lamp/
	ll	bell	/bel/
/m/	m	man	/man/
/n/	n	net	/net/
	nn	inn	/in/
/p/	p	pin	/pin/
/r/	r	rat	/rat/
	rr	err	/er/
/t/	t	top	/top/
	tt	mitt	/mit/
	ed	talked	/tôkt/
/v/	v	van	/van/
/w/	w	web	/web/
/y/	y	yell	/yel/
/f/	f	fine	/fīn/
	ff	cuff	/kuf/

Consonant Sounds	Spellings	Examples	Sound-Spellings
/f/	ph	phone	/fōn/
	gh	rough	/ruf/
/j/	j	jail	/jāl/
	g (e, i, y)	gem	/jem/
	dge	edge	/ej/
/k/	c	cane	/kān/
	k	kite	/kīt/
	ck	kick	/kik/
	ch	ache	/āk/
/s/	s	sent	/sent/
	ss	pass	/pas/
	c (e, i, y)	cent	/sent/
	sc (e, i, y)	scent	/sent/
/z/	z	graze	/grāz/
	zz	buzz	/buz/
	s	raise	/rāz/
/sh/	sh	ship	/ship/
	ch	chute	/shüt/
/ch/	ch	chop	/chop/
	tch	match	/mach/
/th/	th	thin	/thin/
/ᴛʜ/	th	them	/ᴛʜem/
/ng/	ng	sing	/sing/
	n(k)	sink	/singk/
	n(c)	zinc	/zingk/
/h/ /w/	wh	whale	/hwāl/
/k/ /w/	qu	quit	/kwit/
/k/ /s/	cks	tacks	/taks/
	x	box	/boks/

Vowels

Vowel Sounds	Spellings	Examples	Sound-Spellings
/a/	a	hat	/hat/
/e/	e	ten	/ten/
/i/	i	pin	/pin/
/o/	o	mop	/mop/
/u/	u	sun	/sun/
/ā/	ai	train	/trān/
	ay	tray	/trā/
	a-*consonant*-e	grape	/grāp/
/ē/	e	me	/mē/
	ee	heel	/hēl/
	ea	heal	/hēl/
	e-*consonant*-e	eve	/ēv/
/ī/	y	try	/trī/
	i(gh)	bright	/brīt/
	i(nd)	blind	/blīnd/
	ie	tie	/tī/
	i-*consonant*-e	mile	/mīl/
/ō/	o	go	/gō/
	o(ld)	hold	/hōld/
	oa	boat	/bōt/
	oe	toe	/tō/
	ow	tow	/tō/
	o-*consonant*-e	note	/nōt/
/ū/ *or*	ue	glue	/glü/
/ü/	ui	suit	/süt/
	ew	new	/nü/
	u-*consonant*-e	mule	/mūl/

Vowel Sounds	Spellings	Examples	Sound-Spellings
/ü/	oo	moon	/mün/
/u̇/	oo	book	/bu̇k/
/oi/	oy	boy	/boi/
	oi	oil	/oil/
/ou/	ou	mouth	/mouth/
	ow	down	/doun/
/ô/	o	moth	/môth/
	aw	law	/lô/
	au	haul	/hôl/
	a(l)	hall	/hôl/
/är/	ar	star	/stär/
/ãr/	are	care	/kãr/
	air	hair	/hãr/
/ôr/	or	for	/fôr/
	ore	more	/môr/
	oar	roar	/rôr/
/ėr/	er	her	/hėr/
	ir	sir	/sėr/
	ur	fur	/fėr/
/ir/	ear	dear	/dir/
	eer	cheer	/chir/

Mastery Test 1

A

Write a regular spelling for each of these sound-spellings.

1 /thrō/
2 /gông/
3 /hō/
4 /fėrn/
5 /snuf/
6 /nu̇k/
7 /krôs/
8 /chėrn/
9 /kwānt/
10 /krü/
11 /shokt/
12 /yärd/
13 /krangk/
14 /vôlt/
15 /skwãr/
16 /klā/
17 /hwēl/
18 /ŦHēz/
19 /gril/
20 /bôld/
21 /hôk/
22 /shī/
23 /noch/
24 /rīs/
25 /wej/
26 /chãr/
27 /skōld/
28 /floks/
29 /chēp/
30 /fuz/
31 /dans/
32 /his/
33 /join/
34 /grīnd/
35 /früt/
36 /züm/
37 /toiz/
38 /kôrd/
39 /brīt/
40 /glü/
41 /hound/
42 /stāj/
43 /môr/
44 /thėrd/
45 /krīd/
46 /hôrd/
47 /froun/
48 /ôf/

B

Write the sentences, using regular spelling and correct capitalization and punctuation.

1 /ŦHis/ /fōn/ /stil/ /māks/ /tü/ /much/ /noiz/ /hwen/ /it/ /ringz/

2 /ēch/ /akt/ /in/ /our/ /skül/ /plā/ /haz/ /thrē/ /shôrt/ /sēnz/

3 /ŦHēz/ /līnz/ /ôn/ /mī/ /graf/ /shō/ /hou/ /much/ /grān/ /wē/ /sōld/ /last/ /wēk/

4 /ŦHat/ /kwāl/ /bī/ /our/ /hej/ /haz/ /broun/ /spots/ /ôn/ /its/ /bak/

5 /stif/ /strô/ /hėrts/ /mī/ /bãr/ /fēt/

6 /hē/ /ōnz/ /fīv/ /blü/ /süts/ /and/ /siks/ /nü/ /pingk/ /shėrts/

7 /kīnd/ /boiz/ /wil/ /help/ /us/ /hôl/ /briks/ /in/ /ᴛʜat/ /hūj/ /van/

8 /just/ /sit/ /in/ /ᴛʜə/ /fresh/ /ãr/ /hwīl/ /ī/ /gō/ /fôr/ /mī/ /kōt/

9 /ī/ /mīt/ /ūz/ /ᴛʜis/ /lông/ /bôrd/ /hwen/ /ī/ /fiks/ /mī/ /fens/

10 /shē/ /wil/ /stich/ /hėr/ /hwīt/ /wu̇l/ /dres/ /with/ /brīt/ /red/ /yärn/

11 /nou/ /it/ /iz/ /nün/ /in/ /our/ /tīm/ /zōn/

12 /ôl/ /stôrz/ /in/ /toun/ /sel/ /egz/ /and/ /milk/ /at/ /kôst/

Additional Skill Drills

Do these skill drills to improve your Mastery Test score.

Additional Skill Drill 1 Write a regular spelling for each of these one-syllable short-vowel verbs. Use the charts on pages 13-16 to help you spell the words. Check your answers at the end of Chapter 1.

Additional Skill Drill 2 Write the regular spellings for these picture words. All the words are long-vowel words. Use the charts in the chapter to help you write the words. Check your answers at the end of Chapter 1.

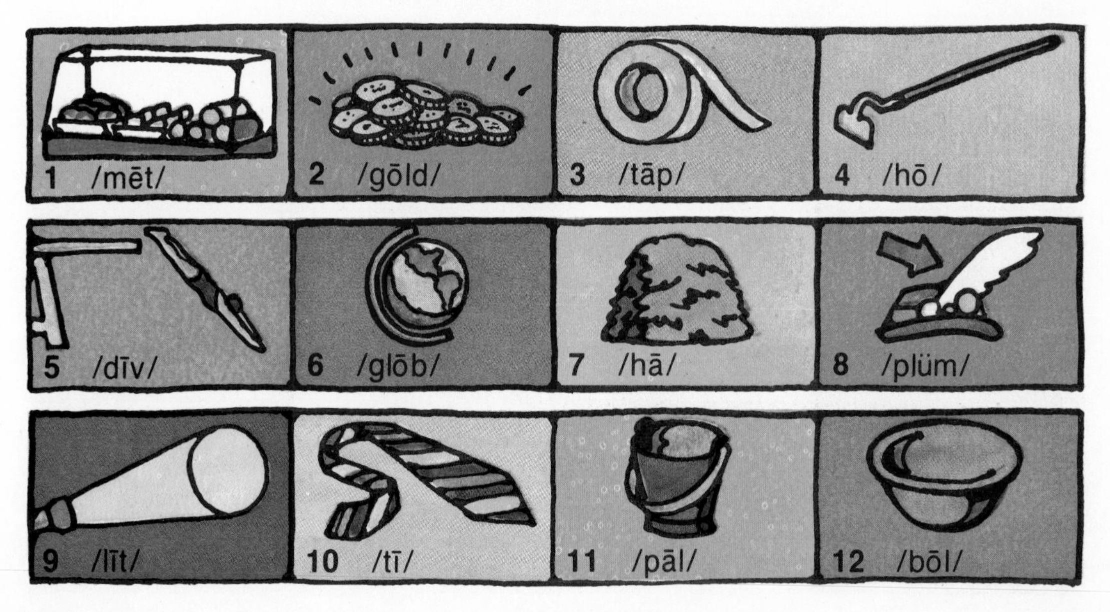

Additional Skill Drill 3 Write the regular spellings for these picture words. Check your answers.

Additional Skill Drill 4 Write the regular spellings for these picture words. Check your answers.

Additional Skill Drill 5 Write the regular spellings for these picture words that have vowel-*r* spellings. Check your answers.

Answers for Chapter 1 Skill Drills

Skill Drill 1 Answers

1 ram 2 trap 3 lamp 4 ramp 5 wig 6 lid 7 blimp 8 tug 9 peg 10 mug 11 vent 12 pond 13 plug 14 pig 15 bulb 16 hump 17 belt 18 hand 19 tent 20 tag

Skill Drill 2 Answers

Be sure you have an example word for each spelling option. Some possibilities are listed here. If you have other answers, check them in a dictionary. 1 *ai,* grain 2 *ay,* pray 3 *a*-consonant-*e*, tape 4 *e,* be 5 *ee,* feel 6 *ea,* steal 7 *e*-consonant-*e*, these 8 *y*, my 9 *i(gh),* fright 10 *i(nd),* kind 11 *ie,* die 12 *i*-consonant-*e*, prize 13 *o,* no 14 *o(ld),* bold 15 *oa,* float 16 *oe,* doe 17 *ow,* throw 18 *o*-consonant-*e*, vote 19 *ue,* sue 20 *ui,* bruise 21 *ew,* flew 22 *u*-consonant-*e,* duke

Skill Drill 3 Answers

1 brain 2 bead 3 light 4 tribe 5 grow 6 pole 7 dune 8 rule 9 bone 10 ray 11 hate 12 deed 13 pry 14 bind 15 hold 16 woe 17 true 18 tube 19 brew 20 pie 21 goal

Skill Drill 4 Answers

1 grain 2 mean 3 dry 4 tight 5 bold 6 moan *or* mown 7 true 8 drew 9 day 10 green 11 pave 12 grind 13 pride 14 lied 15 blow 16 hope 17 rude 18 prune 19 toe *or* tow 20 aim 21 dream

Skill Drill 5 Answers

Be sure you have an example for each spelling option. Some possibilities are listed here. If you have other answers, check them in a dictionary. 1 *f,* far 2 *ph,* graph 3 *gh,* enough 4 *j,* jump 5 *g,* gentle 6 *dge,* judge 7 *c,* cast 8 *k,* key 9 *ck,* lock 10 *ch,* anchor 11 *s,* sell 12 *c,* cereal 13 *sc,* scene 14 *z,* lazy 15 *s,* praise

Skill Drill 6 Answers

Be sure you have an example for each spelling option, except numbers 2 and 9. Some possibilities are listed here. If you have other answers, check them in a dictionary. 1 *sh,* shelf 2 *ch,* charade 3 *ch,* chief 4 *tch,* catch 5 *th,* thick 6 *th,* than 7 *ng,* string 8 *n(k),* think 9 *n(c),* uncle 10 *wh,* white 11 *qu,* quick 12 *cks,* tracks 13 *x,* fix

Skill Drill 7 Answers

1 foam 2 choke 3 thank 4 tasks 5 latch 6 quail 7 phrase *or* frays 8 huge 9 cape 10 ache 11 hose *or* hoes 12 crush 13 white 14 fix 15 squint 16 joke 17 badge 18 cave 19 stick 20 press 21 thrill 22 cling 23 sticks 24 whiz 25 space 26 face 27 junk 28 them

Skill Drill 8 Answers

1 fright 2 kiss 3 chew 4 quilt 5 necks 6 rough 7 hedge 8 scheme 9 scenes 10 quiz 11 shrill 12 tax *or* tacks 13 rink 14 these 15 speak 16 crime 17 phase *or* faze 18 fuss 19 shack 20 laugh 21 rage 22 squeal 23 chose 24 chef 25 scratch 26 think 27 whine

Skill Drill 9 Answers

Be sure you have an example for each spelling option. Some possibilities are listed here. If you have other answers, check them in a dictionary. 1 *oo,* soon 2 *u*-consonant-*e,* brute 3 *ew,* new 4 *ue,* glue 5 *ui,* fruit 6 *oo,* foot 7 *oy,* joy 8 *oi,* toil 9 *ou,* south 10 *ow,* town 11 *aw,* straw 12 *au,* fault 13 *a(l),* salt

Skill Drill 10 Answers

1 fool 2 halt 3 hawk 4 swoop 5 boy 6 fault 7 coil 8 spout 9 scowl 10 launch 11 yawn 12 brook

Skill Drill 11 Answers

1 school 2 crook 3 scald 4 claw 5 cool 6 count 7 joy 8 point 9 crowd 10 haunt 11 sprawl 12 vault

Skill Drill 12 Answers

Be sure you have an example for each spelling option. Some possibilities are listed below. If you have other answers, check the dictionary. 1 *ar,* marsh 2 *are,* stare 3 *air,* stair 4 *or,* nor 5 *ore,* store 6 *oar,* board 7 *er,* fern 8 *ir,* stir 9 *ur,* burn 10 *ear,* near 11 *eer,* deer

Skill Drill 13 Answers

1 scorch 2 share 3 steer 4 burn 5 scarf 6 lair 7 core 8 board *or* bored 9 verb 10 squirm 11 rear 12 whirl 13 churn 14 square 15 third

Skill Drill 14 Answers

1 squirt 2 sneer 3 harsh 4 spare 5 sport 6 curb 7 smear 8 germ 9 coarse 10 snore 11 scare 12 chore 13 chair 14 stores 15 score

Answers for Chapter 1 Additional Skill Drills

Additional Skill Drill 1 Answers

1 punt 2 bend 3 drop 4 mend 5 print 6 bunt *or* hit *or* bat 7 dig 8 wed

Additional Skill Drill 2 Answers

1 meat 2 gold 3 tape 4 hoe 5 dive 6 globe 7 hay 8 plume 9 light 10 tie 11 pail 12 bowl 13 wind 14 feet 15 vine 16 braid

Additional Skill Drill 3 Answers

1 phone 2 bell 3 lock 4 crutch 5 queen 6 ax *or* axe 7 cake 8 slice 9 fuse 10 snail 11 whale 12 king 13 tracks 14 jail 15 stage 16 shell 17 coach 18 wink 19 chess 20 chef 21 graph 22 gym 23 judge 24 scale

Additional Skill Drill 4 Answers

1 stool 2 cook 3 shawl 4 spoon 5 toy 6 hound
7 coin 8 vault 9 clown 10 saw 11 coil 12 frown

Additional Skill Drill 5 Answers

1 deer 2 chair 3 shark 4 score 5 churn 6 shirt
7 spear 8 oar 9 fern 10 square 11 torch 12 cork

2 Consonant Ghosts and Snurks

In Chapter 1 you reviewed the usual spelling options for our sounds. But sometimes you do not spell words with those spelling options. Words with unexpected spellings we call *snurks.* In some of these words we use consonant letters that spell no sounds at all—the "ghost" letters. In other words there are unexpected spellings for vowel sounds. These are the real snurks in our spellings. This chapter reviews both silent-consonant spellings and snurk spellings.

The Ghost Symbols: Lost Consonant Sounds

A sensible system of spelling should have one symbol for one sound. As there are more sounds than letters in our alphabet, the English spelling is harder than it should be. Our speech—the sounds we make—changes through the years. Our spellings usually do not change. When we stop using certain sounds, we usually keep the same old letters in our spellings. We often call these letters that no longer spell sounds "silent" letters. Some of these silent letters are consonant symbols.

1 The Strange Case of the *gh*

Many years ago people used a consonant sound that is hard to make. It sounded something like a blending of the /k/ and /h/ sounds—as though a speaker were clearing his or her throat. They used *h* to spell this sound. Later the spelling was changed to *gh.* Then people simply stopped using this /kh/ sound. In a few words the /kh/ became an /f/. We still say the /f/ sound for the *gh* spelling in words like *cough* /kôf/, *laugh* /laf/, *rough* /ruf/, *tough* /tuf/, and *draught* /draft/. In many other words the /kh/ consonant sound disappeared but the *gh* spelling was kept. For example, we have the silent *gh* spelling in *caught* /kôt/ and *taught* /tôt/, in *straight* /strāt/, and in *plough* /plou/, *bough* /bou/, and *drought* /drout/.

When *i* comes before *gh* in one-syllable words like these, then *igh* spells /ī/.

high /hī/	fight /fīt/	plight /plīt/
sigh /sī/	flight /flīt/	right /rīt/
thigh /thī/	fright /frīt/	sight /sīt/
nigh /nī/	light /līt/	slight /slīt/
blight /blīt/	might /mīt/	tight /tīt/
bright /brīt/	night /nīt/	

The letters *gh* spell other sounds too. There are some *gh* spellings of /g/ at the beginning of words like *ghost* /gōst/. The reason for this can be traced to Dutch printers. Printing was invented in Germany. When an Englishman, William Caxton, brought a printing press to London, he had to bring over some Dutch printers. As the Dutch spelled the beginning /g/ sound with *gh,* some of these *gh* spellings got into English spelling.

Skill Drill 1 Write the missing *gh* words. Use words from the list above. Check your answers with those at the end of the chapter.

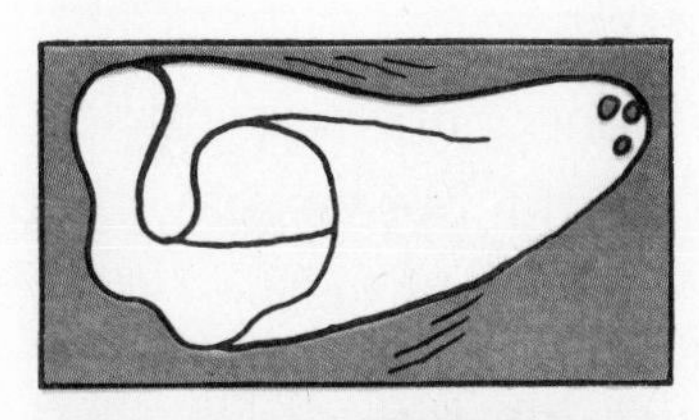

1 This is a ___ in ___.

2 That is a ___ ___!

2 *kn* Spelling /n/

Many years ago English speakers used many words that began with the /kn/ sounds, and they naturally spelled them *kn.* But as the /kn/ sounds are hard for most English speakers to say, the /k/ sound gradually dropped out. But we have kept the *kn* spelling in one-syllable words like these.

knee /nē/	known /nōn/	knot /not/
kneel /nēl/	knife /nīf/	knit /nit/
knelt /nelt/	knives /nīvz/	knave /nāv/
knew /nü/	knight /nīt/	knob /nob/
know /nō/	knock /nok/	knead /nēd/

Skill Drill 2 Write the missing *kn* words. Check your answers at the end of the chapter.

1 This ___ is ___ before the queen.

2 That's a ___ ___ on the door.

3 *wr* Spelling /r/

People once spoke two consonant sounds for the letters *wr.* We no longer say the *w* sound, but we have kept the *wr* spelling in words like these.

wrap /rap/	wrist /rist/	wrath /rath/
wreck /rek/	write /rīt/	wreath /rēth/
wrench /rench/	wrote /rōt/	wreathe /rēᴛʜ/
wring /ring/	wrong /rông/	wretch /rech/
wrung /rung/	wren /ren/	

Skill Drill 3 Write the missing *wr* words.

1 This __ is perched on a __!

2 He certainly __ the word __ the __ way!

4 *gn* Spelling /n/

Speakers once pronounced both the /g/ and the /n/ sounds in words that they spelled with *gn*. The /g/ is no longer pronounced but has become silent. Here are some words that begin with the spelling *gn* but with the sound /n/.

gnaw /nô/	gnarl /närl/	gnash /nash/
gnat /nat/	gnome /nōm/	

Skill Drill 4 Write the missing *gn* words.

That __ is __ his teeth.

5 *mb* Spelling /m/

The /m/ and the /b/ sounds are awkward to say together at the end of a word, and so the *mb* endings are now pronounced /m/. The *b*'s have become silent in words like these.

dumb /dum/	comb /kōm/	climb /klīm/
thumb /thum/	crumb /krum/	tomb /tüm/
bomb /bom/	numb /num/	
lamb /lam/	limb /lim/	

Skill Drill 5 Write the missing *mb* words.

1 Rosa's __ must be __.

2 Stan is __ his pet __.

6 Silent *l*'s

The *l*'s are silent in the *alf* words like *half* /haf/ and *calf* /kaf/, but not in *elf* words like *self* /self/ and *shelf* /shelf/. They are also silent in *calves* /kavz/ and *halves* /havz/ but not in *solve* /solv/.

The *l* is silent in *alm* words like *calm* /käm/, *palm* /päm/, and *balm* /bäm/, but not in *elm* /elm/ and *film* /film/.

The *l* is silent in *alk* words like *walk, talk, chalk, stalk, balk,* and *calk,* and in *olk* words like *yolk* and *folk,* but not in *ilk* words like *silk* and *milk,* nor in *ulk* words like *bulk* and *sulk.*

Skill Drill 6 Write the missing words. All of them are in the paragraphs above.

1 She's __ a __ young __.

2 Let's make a __ of the __ dance.

7 The *tch* and *dge* Spellings

There are many *tch* and *dge* spellings at the ends of one-syllable words.

We may say that *tch* is a common spelling for the dictionary's /ch/ symbol. But the /ch/ symbol really represents *two* consonant sounds: /t/ and /sh/. So the dictionary might show the pronunciation of *catch* as /katsh/ instead of /kach/. Then we might say the *t* in *catch* is silent because the *ch* itself spells /tsh/. Remember to include *t*'s in words like these.

itch	notch	scratch
ditch	hutch	snatch
batch	stitch	clutch
catch	pitch	witch
latch	stretch	twitch
match	snitch	thatch
patch	hitch	watch
fetch	hatch	
crutch	switch	

Skill Drill 7 Write the missing *tch* words.

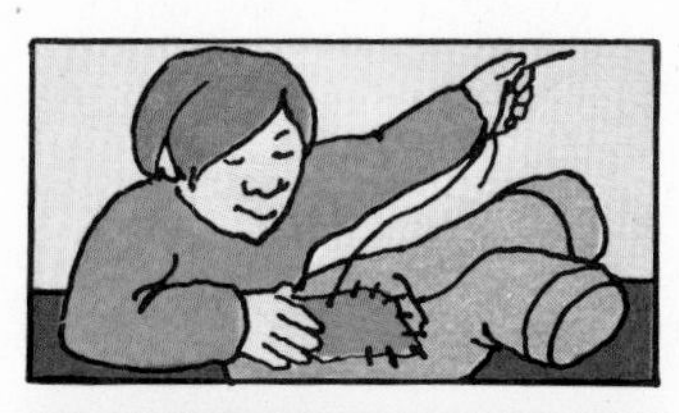

1 Tony is __ a __ on his pants.

2 That __ is scratching an __.

We can also say that the *dge* is a common spelling of the sound the dictionary shows as /j/. The dictionary /j/ is really a symbol for *two* consonant sounds. When you say *edge,* which the dictionary shows as /ej/, you say /e/ and /d/ and a third consonant sound. The third consonant sound is spelled *s* in *measure* and *ge* at the end of *garage*. Dictionaries show this consonant sound as /zh/. The dictionary symbol /j/, then, is really /d/ and/zh/. The dictionaries could show the pronunciation of *edge* as /edzh/ instead of as /ej/. So you might say that the *d*'s are silent in words like *edge* because the *ge* itself spells the /dzh/ sounds. Remember the *d*'s in *dge* words like these.

trudge	dredge	ledge
badge	judge	grudge
hedge	bridge	smudge
ridge	pledge	wedge
lodge	edge	sledge
budge	fudge	drudge
dodge	nudge	sludge

Skill Drill 8 Write the missing *dge* words.

1 They're __ the __.

2 The __ has a __ on his face.

8 Odds and Ends

There are also silent consonant letters in these words.

rhyme /rīm/	debt /det/	whoop /hüp/
hour /our/	sword /sôrd/	
doubt /dout/	sign /sīn/	

Skill Drill 9 Write the missing silent-consonant words.

No ___ she's paying a large ___.

Skill Drill 10 Write the words for these sound-spellings. Refer to the lists in the chapter. Check your answers at the end of Chapter 2.

1 /num/
2 /kaf/
3 /hüp/
4 /tôt/
5 /slīt/
6 /nash/
7 /rist/
8 /käm/
9 /strech/
10 /dout/
11 /nit/
12 /nī/
13 /bôk/
14 /sīn/
15 /gruj/
16 /fōk/
17 /tīt/
18 /blīt/

Skill Drill 11 Write the silent-consonant words for these sound-spellings. Check your answers.

1 /loj/
2 /rīm/
3 /yōk/
4 /drout/
5 /rek/
6 /nô/
7 /bäm/
8 /swich/
9 /sôrd/
10 /strāt/
11 /krum/
12 /haf/
13 /sī/
14 /nob/
15 /frīt/
16 /kôk/
17 /drej/
18 /det/

Snurks!

You have learned that when you *hear* certain sounds in one-syllable words, you can expect to *see* certain spellings. But there are words with unexpected spellings—snurks. A snurk is a word that is not spelled as you would expect it to be spelled. When you look at any word, notice whether it is spelled as you would expect it to be spelled. If it is not, notice *how* it differs from the expected spelling. Words with snurk spellings are shown in this book with the ▽ symbol.

1 Short-Vowel Snurks

You have learned that short-vowel sounds are usually spelled *a, e, i, o,* and *u.* Study the short-vowel sound-spellings in these one-syllable words. All these words are snurks because they do not have expected *a, e, i, o,* or *u* spellings. For example, you would expect /hav/ to be spelled *hav.* You would expect *have* to spell /hāv/ instead of /hav/. You would expect /laf/ to be spelled *laf.* You would expect the *au* in *laugh* to spell /ô/ and the *gh* to be silent. You would expect the *a's* in *shall, valve,* and *scalp* to spell /ô/. You would expect the *ai* in *plaid* to spell /ā/ instead of /a/.

/a/ Snurks		Sound-Spellings	
▽ have	▽ valve	/hav/	/valv/
▽ laugh	▽ scalp	/laf/	/skalp/
▽ shall	▽ plaid	/shal/	/plad/

Skill Drill 12 Write the missing /a/ snurks.

They're __ at his __ __.

/e/ Snurks	Sound-Spellings	/e/ Snurks	Sound-Spellings
▽ head	/hed/	▽ death	/deth/
▽ dead	/ded/	▽ meant	/ment/
▽ read*	/red/	▽ sweat	/swet/
▽ lead*	/led/	▽ wealth	/welth/
▽ dread	/dred/	▽ dealt	/delt/
▽ bread	/bred/	▽ friend	/frend/
▽ thread	/thred/	▽ says	/sez/
▽ spread	/spred/	▽ said	/sed/
▽ breath	/breth/	▽ guess	/ges/

*When *read* is pronounced /rēd/ and when *lead* is pronounced /lēd/, the spellings are regular.

Skill Drill 13 Write the missing /e/ snurks.

1 There's __ in his __!

2 His __ is a man of great __.

/i/ Snurks	Sound-Spellings	/i/ Snurks	Sound-Spellings
been	/bin/	sieve	/siv/
live*	/liv/	build	/bild/
give	/giv/	built	/bilt/

*When *live* is pronounced /līv/, the spelling is regular.

/o/ and /ô/ Snurks	Sound-Spellings	/o/ and /ô/ Snurks	Sound-Spellings
what	/hwot/	yacht	/yot/
wash	/wosh/	gone	/gôn/
want	/wont/	ought	/ôt/
wasp	/wosp/	bought	/bôt/
swan	/swon/	fought	/fôt/
swap	/swop/	brought	/brôt/
swamp	/swomp/	thought	/thôt/
squat	/skwot/	cough	/kôf/
squash	/skwosh/	trough	/trôf/

Skill Drill 14 Write the missing /i/, /o/, and /ô/ snurks.

1 That house has __ badly __.

2 That __ has a bad __.

3 He's __ the __ out of the pigs' __.

/u/ Snurks	Sound-Spellings	/u/ Snurks	Sound-Spellings
son	/sun/	love	/luv/
ton	/tun/	dove*	/duv/
won	/wun/	shove	/shuv/
from	/frum/	glove	/gluv/
front	/frunt/	does	/duz/
month	/munth/	blood	/blud/
once	/wuns/	flood	/flud/
sponge	/spunj/	rough	/ruf/
one	/wun/	tough	/tuf/
done	/dun/	touch	/tuch/
none	/nun/	young	/yung/

*When *dove* is pronounced /dōv/, the spelling is regular.

Skill Drill 15 Write the missing /u/ snurks.

1 That __ old __ is __ fighter!

2 He lost __ of his __.

Skill Drill 16 Read these sound-spellings. Write the spellings for the short-vowel snurks. Use the charts of short-vowel snurks to help you. Check your answers at the end of Chapter 2.

1 /luv/	**10** /shuv/	**19** /frend/
2 /welth/	**11** /wuns/	**20** /sed/
3 /hav/	**12** /deth/	**21** /thôt/
4 /bôt/	**13** /skalp/	**22** /frunt/
5 /ruf/	**14** /dun/	**23** /swop/
6 /blud/	**15** /tuch/	**24** /spred/
7 /hwot/	**16** /wont/	**25** /tun/
8 /ded/	**17** /bild/	**26** /gôn/
9 /skwot/	**18** /yung/	**27** /tred/

Skill Drill 17 Write the spellings for these short-vowel snurks. Use the charts to help you. Check your answers at the end of Chapter 2.

1 /shal/	**10** /delt/	**19** /dred/
2 /valv/	**11** /hed/	**20** /wosh/
3 /tuf/	**12** /sez/	**21** /breth/
4 /kum/	**13** /ges/	**22** /flud/
5 /bilt/	**14** /thred/	**23** /duz/
6 /ment/	**15** /wosp/	**24** /skwosh/
7 /swomp/	**16** /munth/	**25** /ôt/
8 /trôf/	**17** /gluv/	**26** /nun/
9 /frum/	**18** /giv/	**27** /brôt/

2 Long-Vowel Snurks

Because there are more vowel *sounds* than vowel symbols in our alphabet, we have to use vowel-symbol combinations. The vowel letters *a, e, i, o,* and *u* often spell the short vowel sounds. There are several spelling patterns for each of the long vowel sounds, as you saw in Chapter 1. Review the charts on pages 13-16. These are the spellings you expect to see in one-syllable long-vowel words.

Long-Vowel Spelling Patterns

/ā/	/ē/	/ī/
ai (fail)	e (me)	ie (pie)
ay (say)	ea (tea)	y (sky)
a-*consonant*-e (cake).	ee (keep)	i(gh) (high)
	e-*consonant*-e (these)	i(nd) (mind)
		i-*consonant*-e (mile)

/ō/	/ū/ or /ü/
o (so)	ue (blue)
oa (boat)	ui (suit)
ow (low)	ew (few)
o(ld) (cold)	u-*consonant*-e (mule)
o-*consonant*-e (pole)	

Study these lists of long-vowel snurks, which are not spelled as you would expect them to be spelled. Read the words. Notice that the spelling options are not those you studied in Chapter 1.

/ā/ Snurks	Sound-Spellings	/ā/ Snurks	Sound-Spellings
bass*	/bās/	sleigh	/slā/
paste	/pāst/	beige	/bāzh/
taste	/tāst/	freight	/frāt/
waste	/wāst/	veil	/vāl/
haste	/hāst/	vein	/vān/
break	/brāk/	prey	/prā/
great	/grāt/	they	/ŦHā/
steak	/stāk/	hey	/hā/
rein	/rān/	vague	/vāg/
weigh	/wā/	plague	/plāg/
weight	/wāt/	gauge	/gāj/
neigh	/nā/		

*When *bass* is pronounced /bas/, it is not a snurk.

Skill Drill 18 Write the missing /ā/ snurks for the sentences below. Use /ā/ snurks from the list. Check your answers at the end of Chapter 2.

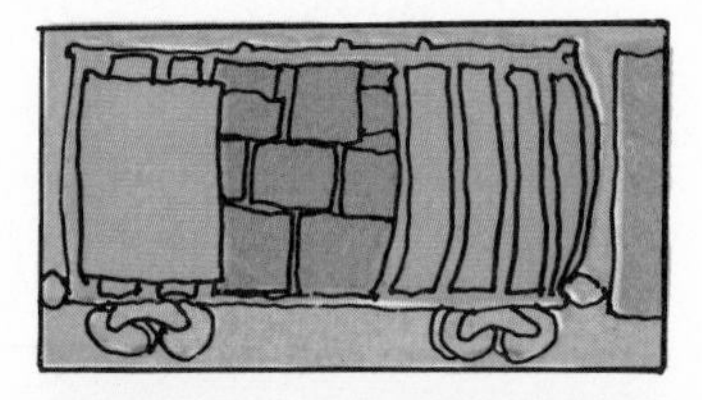

1 The __ had too much __.

2 That __ drum is going to __!

/ē/ Snurks	Sound-Spellings	/ē/ Snurks	Sound-Spellings
field	/fēld/	piece	/pēs/
yield	/yēld/	niece	/nēs/
shield	/shēld/	siege	/sēj/
grief	/grēf/	priest	/prēst/
brief	/brēf/	shriek	/shrēk/
thief	/thēf/	fiend	/fēnd/
grieve	/grēv/	wield	/wēld/
thieves	/thēvz/	ski	/skē/

Skill Drill 19 Write the missing /ē/ snurks.

1 The __ will __ to the man with the __.

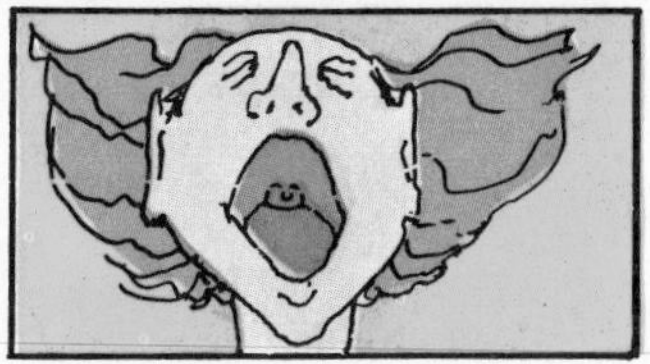

2 That __ is __ rather loudly.

/ī/ Snurks	Sound-Spellings	/ī/ Snurks	Sound-Spellings
▽ child	/chīld/	▽ guide	/gīd/
▽ wild	/wīld/	▽ ninth	/nīnth/
▽ mild	/mīld/	▽ pint	/pīnt/
▽ guy	/gī/	▽ height	/hīt/
▽ buy	/bī/	▽ eye	/ī/

/ō/ Snurks	Sound-Spellings	/ō/ Snurks	Sound-Spellings
▽ most	/mōst/	▽ stroll	/strōl/
▽ host	/hōst/	▽ scroll	/skrōl/
▽ post	/pōst/	▽ soul	/sōl/
▽ colt	/kōlt/	▽ dough	/dō/
▽ both	/bōth/	▽ though	/ŧʜō/
▽ roll	/rōl/	▽ rogue	/rōg/
▽ poll	/pōl/	▽ sew	/sō/

Skill Drill 20 Write the missing /ī/ and /ō/ snurks.

1 Now that's a __ of great __!

2 That __ will never steal that __!

/ū/ and /ü/ Snurks	Sound-Spellings	/ū/ and /ü/ Snurks	Sound-Spellings
▽ you	/ū/	▽ whom	/hüm/
▽ youth	/ūth/	▽ whose	/hüz/
▽ view	/vū/	▽ move	/müv/
▽ feud	/fūd/	▽ prove	/prüv/
▽ shoe	/shü/	▽ lose	/lüz/

/ū/ and /ü/ Snurks	Sound-Spellings	/ū/ and /ü/ Snurks	Sound-Spellings
soup	/süp/	truth	/trüth/
group	/grüp/	route*	/rüt/
through	/thrü/	wound*	/wünd/
who	/hü/	rouge	/rüzh/

*When *route* is pronounced /rout/, it is not a snurk. When *wound* is pronounced /wound/, it is not a snurk.

Skill Drill 21 Write the missing /ū/ and /ü/ snurks.

1 This __ really likes __.

2 It's a __ about a __.

Skill Drill 22 Write the long-vowel snurks for these sound-spellings. Use the lists in the chapter to help you spell the words. Check your answers.

1 /trüth/
2 /kōlt/
3 /nēs/
4 /ŧʜā/
5 /wīld/
6 /vāg/
7 /fēld/
8 /mōst/
9 /hāst/
10 /gī/
11 /bōth/
12 /lüz/
13 /vū/
14 /fūd/
15 /wünd/
16 /brēf/
17 /shrēk/
18 /rōg/
19 /thēvz/
20 /gīd/
21 /bāzh/
22 /mīld/
23 /grēv/
24 /yēld/
25 /plāg/
26 /müv/
27 /hīt/
28 /wēld/
29 /strōl/
30 /grēf/
31 /ūth/
32 /grüp/
33 /rüzh/
34 /sēj/
35 /ŧʜō/
36 /tāst/

Skill Drill 23 Write these long-vowel snurks.

1 /hü/	**10** /süp/	**19** /nā/
2 /vān/	**11** /wā/	**20** /pēs/
3 /prā/	**12** /grāt/	**21** /hüz/
4 /rān/	**13** /thrü/	**22** /rüt/
5 /brāk/	**14** /rōl/	**23** /pōl/
6 /bī/	**15** /shü/	**24** /wāst/
7 /prüv/	**16** /hā/	**25** /hüm/
8 /sōl/	**17** /stāk/	**26** /dō/
9 /ū/	**18** /bās/	

3 The /u̇/ Snurks

As you saw in Chapter 1, there are several two-letter combinations that spell vowel sounds.

Two-Letter Vowel Spellings

/ü/	/ou/	/oi/	/ô/
oo (moon)	ou (loud)	oy (boy)	aw (saw)
/u̇/	ow (crowd)	oi (oil)	au (haul)
oo (book)			a(l) (ball)

The /ü/ snurks are included in the snurk list on pages 40-41. The /ô/ snurks are included in the list on page 35. There are no /ou/ snurks, since the /ou/ sound is always spelled *ou* or *ow*. There are no /oi/ snurks, since the /oi/ sound is always spelled *oy* or *oi*. We expect the /u̇/ vowel sound to be spelled *oo*. Here are the /u̇/ snurks.

/u̇/ Snurks	Sound-Spellings	/u̇/ Snurks	Sound-Spellings
▽ could	/ku̇d/	▽ bull	/bu̇l/
▽ would	/wu̇d/	▽ bush	/bu̇sh/
▽ should	/shu̇d/	▽ push	/pu̇sh/
▽ put	/pu̇t/	▽ wolf	/wu̇lf/
▽ full	/fu̇l/	▽ wolves	/wu̇lvz/

Skill Drill 24 Write the /u̇/ snurks for these sound-spellings. Check your answers.

1 /pu̇t/	**4** /wu̇lf/	**7** /pu̇sh/
2 /ku̇d/	**5** /shu̇d/	**8** /wu̇lvz/
3 /bu̇sh/	**6** /bu̇l/	**9** /fu̇l/

4 The Vowel-*r* Snurks

In Chapter 1 you studied vowel-*r* spellings. The regular spelling options for vowel-*r* words are reviewed in the chart below. Study these to be sure of the regular spellings. Notice that two additional sounds and spellings are included. After reading this chart, study the vowel-*r* snurks in the following lists.

Vowel-*r* Sound-Spellings	Regular Spellings	Examples	Sound-Spellings
/är/	ar	star	/stär/
/ãr/	are	care	/kãr/
	air	hair	/hãr/
/ôr/	or	for	/fôr/
	ore	more	/môr/
	oar	roar	/rôr/
/ėr/	er	her	/hėr/
	ir	sir	/sėr/
	ur	fur	/fėr/
/ir/	ear	dear	/dir/
	eer	cheer	/chir/
There are also these vowel-*r* spellings.			
/our/	our	sour	/sour/
/u̇r/	oor	poor	/pu̇r/

Study these lists of vowel-*r* snurks. What are the unexpected spellings that make them snurks?

/är/ Snurks	Sound-Spellings
▽ are	/är/
▽ heart	/härt/
▽ hearth	/härth/
▽ guard	/gärd/

/ãr/ Snurks	Sound-Spellings	/ãr/ Snurks	Sound-Spellings
▽ there	/ᴛʜãr/	▽ tear*	/tãr/
▽ where	/hwãr/	▽ pear	/pãr/
▽ bear	/bãr/	▽ their	/ᴛʜãr/
▽ wear	/wãr/	▽ heir	/ãr/

*When *tear* is pronounced /tir/, it is not a snurk.

Skill Drill 25 Write the missing /är/ and /ãr/ snurks. Use the lists to help you.

1 Now there's a __ with a big __.

2 You know a __ wouldn't __ that kind of hat!

/ôr/ Snurks	Sound-Spellings	/ôr/ Snurks	Sound-Spellings
▽ four	/fôr/	▽ course	/kôrs/
▽ fourth	/fôrth/	▽ source	/sôrs/
▽ pour	/pôr/	▽ door	/dôr/
▽ court	/kôrt/	▽ floor	/flôr/

/ėr/ Snurks	Sound-Spellings
earn	/ėrn/
earth	/ėrth/
heard	/hėrd/
learn	/lėrn/
yearn	/yėrn/
pearl	/pėrl/
word	/wėrd/

/ėr/ Snurks	Sound-Spellings
work	/wėrk/
worm	/wėrm/
worth	/wėrth/
worse	/wėrs/
were	/wėr/
scourge	/skėrj/

/u̇r/ Snurks	Sound-Spellings
your	/yu̇r/
tour	/tu̇r/
sure	/shu̇r/

Skill Drill 26 Write the missing /ôr/ and /ėr/ snurks.

1 __ judges in one __?

2 Those __ must be __ a lot of money!

Skill Drill 27 Write the snurk words for these sound-spellings. Use the lists of snurks if you need to. Check your answers.

1 /härth/
2 /wėrk/
3 /flôr/
4 /yėrn/
5 /sôrs/
6 /ėrth/
7 /hwãr/
8 /kôrt/
9 /lėrn/
10 /wėr/
11 /wėrd/
12 /wėrth/
13 /wėrs/
14 /skėrj/

Skill Drill 28 Write the snurk words for these sound-spellings. Check your answers.

1 /är/
2 /hėrd/
3 /tãr/
4 /fôr/
5 /kôrs/
6 /ėrn/
7 /ãr/
8 /ŦHãr/
9 /wãr/

Summary

In this chapter you have reviewed words with silent consonant letters and words with unexpected spellings—snurks. Both kinds of words require special attention.

Silent-consonant words are easier to spell if you learn the letter patterns in which the silent consonants usually occur. These are examples of the common silent-consonant-letter spellings.

*k*nee /nē/
wa*l*k /wôk/
thi*gh* /thī/
*w*rite /rīt/
ca*l*m /käm/
com*b* /kōm/
*g*nat /nat/
ha*l*f /haf/
le*d*ge /lej/
de*b*t /det/
pi*t*ch /pich/

Snurks are spelling problems because they are not predictable. The only way to be sure of a snurk spelling is to study each word individually. Snurks are easier to spell if you notice how the snurk spelling differs from the expected spelling.

In this chapter you have studied snurks that are short-vowel words, long-vowel words, two-letter vowel words, and vowel-*r* words. Some examples of the snurks are given below. Notice the unexpected spellings in each of these examples.

/a/ have, scalp
/o/ squash
/ā/ vein, great
/ō/ sew, both
/u̇/ could, bush
/ôr/ pour, door
/e/ bread, guess
/ô/ cough
/ē/ niece, shield
/ū/ youth
/är/ heart, guard
/ėr/ earth, were
/i/ give, build
/u/ front, glove
/ī/ pint, buy
/ü/ prove
/ãr/ there, heir
/u̇r/ your, sure

Mastery Test 2

A

Spell the words correctly. Words with snurk spellings are shown with the ▽ symbol.

1 ▽ /frāt/
2 ▽ /vāg/
3 /klā/
4 /gān/
5 ▽ /bāzh/
6 ▽ /gāj/
7 ▽ /ŦHā/
8 ▽ /tāst/
9 /dāt/
10 ▽ /prēst/
11 ▽ /skē/
12 /strēm/
13 /chēk/
14 /ŦHēz/
15 ▽ /nēs/
16 /trīd/
17 /skī/
18 ▽ /wīld/
19 ▽ /gī/
20 ▽ /gīd/
21 /kwīt/
22 /slīt/
23 ▽ /hīt/
24 ▽ /pīnt/
25 /shō/
26 ▽ /kōlt/
27 ▽ /ŦHō/
28 ▽ /rōg/
29 /skōld/
30 /kōch/
31 ▽ /skrōl/
32 /chōz/
33 ▽ /ūth/
34 ▽ /vū/
35 ▽ /fūd/
36 /früt/
37 /krü/
38 ▽ /shü/
39 ▽ /thrü/
40 /fūm/
41 /kū/
42 ▽ /hüz/
43 ▽ /prüv/
44 ▽ /wünd/
45 ▽ /shu̇r/
46 ▽ /pu̇l/
47 ▽ /tu̇r/
48 /stu̇d/
49 ▽ /ku̇d/
50 ▽ /wu̇lf/
51 ▽ /är/
52 ▽ /härt/
53 /skärf/
54 /chärm/
55 ▽ /gärd/
56 ▽ /härth/
57 ▽ /fôrth/
58 ▽ /sôrs/
59 /pôrt/
60 /rôr/
61 /skôr/
62 ▽ /dôr/
63 ▽ /yėrn/
64 ▽ /skėrj/
65 ▽ /wėr/
66 /bėrn/
67 /hwėrl/
68 ▽ /pėrl/
69 /bėrst/
70 ▽ /wėrth/

B

Spell the silent-letter words.

1 /lam/
2 /nat/
3 /rap/
4 /kaf/
5 /bäm/
6 /baj/
7 /wej/
8 /fech/
9 /det/
10 /rist/
11 /brij/
12 /swich/

13 /lach/	**19** /sôrd/	**25** /dum/
14 /loj/	**20** /rīm/	**26** /sī/
15 /nob/	**21** /thum/	**27** /nash/
16 /nēl/	**22** /nōn/	**28** /our/
17 /rēth/	**23** /nōm/	**29** /hüp/
18 /nē/	**24** /krum/	**30** /drout/

Write the words for the sound-spellings in these sentences.

1 We /ôt/ __ to /klīm/ __ up and trim those /närld/ __ /limz/ __ from the tree.

2 The old /nāv/ __ /nelt/ __ on his /rīt/ __ /nē/ __ to beg pardon for his /rôngz/ __.

3 I /dout/ __ that the /hōl/ __ load of /frāt/ __ /wāz/ __ more than /haf/ __ a ton.

4 He /klucht/ __ the piece of /fuj/ __ he had /snacht/ __ from the pan as he ran /thrü/ __ the room.

5 The /yot/ __ drifted four /ourz/ __ on a /käm/ __ sea without the least /sīn/ __ of trouble.

Additional Skill Drills

Do these skill drills if you want to improve your Mastery Test score.

Additional Skill Drill 1 Write these silent-letter picture words. Check your answers at the end of Chapter 2.

Additional Skill Drill 2 Write the spellings for these short-vowel snurk words. Check your answers.

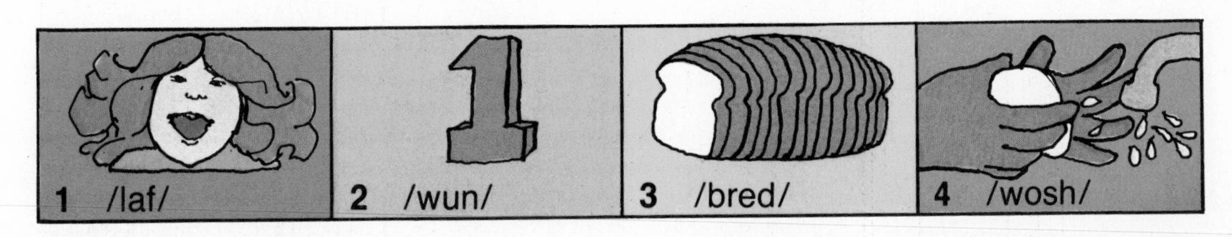

Additional Skill Drill 3 Write the spellings for these long-vowel snurk words. Check your answers.

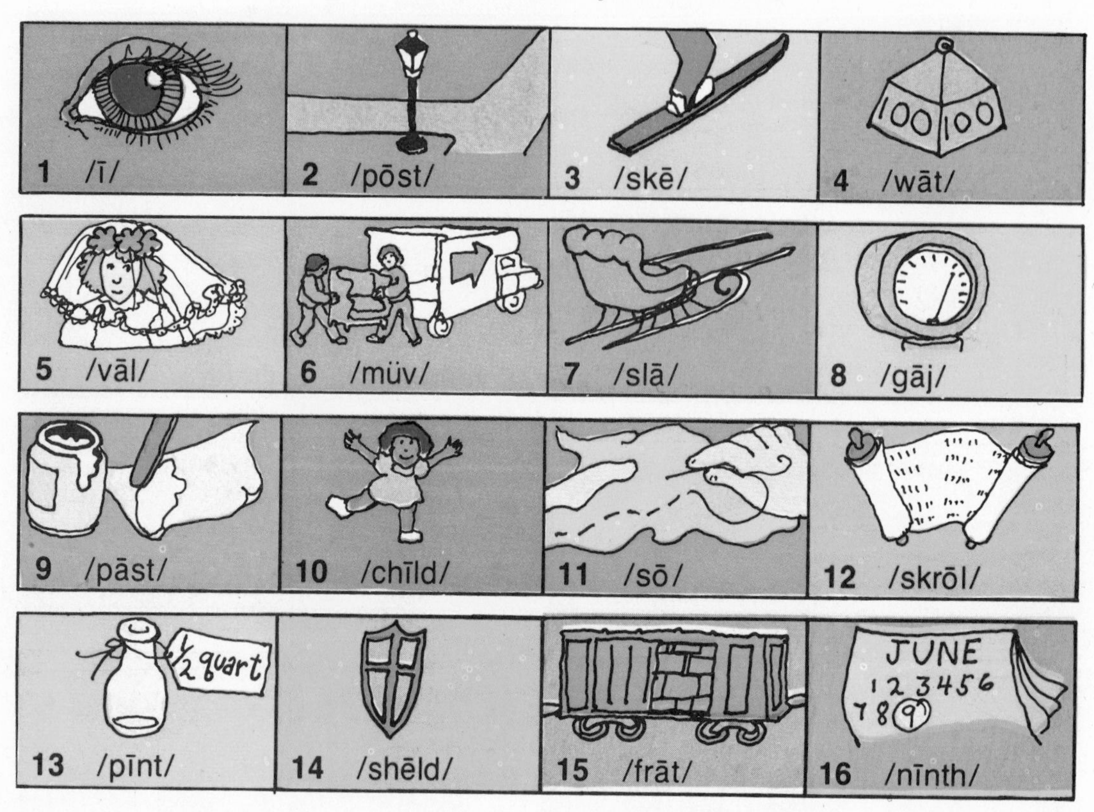

Additional Skill Drill 4 Write the spellings for these vowel-*r* words. Underline the seven words that are not snurks. Check your answers.

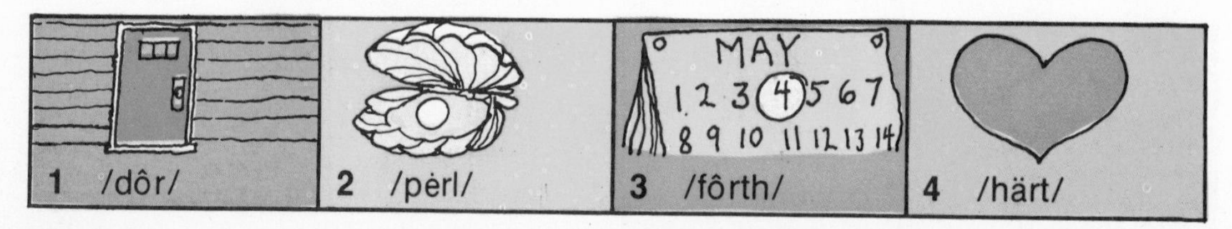

5 /bãr/
6 /wėrm/
7 /pôr/
8 /pãr/
BANK
9 /gärd/
10 /fôr/
11 /flôr/
12 /sour/
13 /kôrt/
14 /rôr/
15 /hãr/
16 /stär/
17 /ėrth/
18 /bėrst/
19 /skärf/
20 /bėrn/
21 /ᴛʜãr/
22 /wãr/
23 /wėrk/
24 /lėrn/

Answers for Chapter 2 Skill Drills

Skill Drill 1 Answers
1 ghost, flight 2 bright, light

Skill Drill 2 Answers
1 knight, kneeling 2 knave, knocking

Skill Drill 3 Answers
1 wren, wreath 2 wrote, wrath, wrong

Skill Drill 4 Answers
gnome, gnashing

Skill Drill 5 Answers
1 limb, numb 2 combing, lamb

Skill Drill 6 Answers
1 stalking, calm, calf 2 film, folk

Skill Drill 7 Answers
1 stitching, patch 2 witch, itch

Skill Drill 8 Answers
1 dredging, sludge 2 judge, smudge

Skill Drill 9 Answers
doubt, debt

Skill Drill 10 Answers
1 numb 2 calf 3 whoop 4 taught 5 slight 6 gnash
7 wrist 8 calm 9 stretch 10 doubt 11 knit 12 nigh
13 balk 14 sign 15 grudge 16 folk 17 tight 18 blight

Skill Drill 11 Answers
1 lodge 2 rhyme 3 yolk 4 drought 5 wreck 6 gnaw
7 balm 8 switch 9 sword 10 straight 11 crumb 12 half
13 sigh 14 knob 15 fright 16 calk 17 dredge 18 debt

Skill Drill 12 Answers
laughing, plaid, scalp

Skill Drill 13 Answers
1 death, breath 2 friend, wealth

Skill Drill 14 Answers
1 been, built 2 swan, cough 3 washing, wasps, trough

Skill Drill 15 Answers
1 tough, dove, some 2 one, gloves

Skill Drill 16 Answers
1 love 2 wealth 3 have 4 bought 5 rough 6 blood
7 what 8 dead 9 squat 10 shove 11 once 12 death
13 scalp 14 done 15 touch 16 want 17 build 18 young
19 friend 20 said 21 thought 22 front 23 swap
24 spread 25 ton 26 gone 27 tread

Skill Drill 17 Answers
1 shall 2 valve 3 tough 4 come 5 built 6 meant
7 swamp 8 trough 9 from 10 dealt 11 head 12 says
13 guess 14 thread 15 wasp 16 month 17 glove
18 give 19 dread 20 wash 21 breath 22 flood 23 does
24 squash 25 ought 26 none 27 brought

Skill Drill 18 Answers
1 freight, weight 2 bass, break

Skill Drill 19 Answers
1 thieves, yield, shield 2 fiend, shrieking

Skill Drill 20 Answers
1 child, height 2 rogue, colt

Skill Drill 21 Answers
1 youth, soup 2 feud, shoe

Skill Drill 22 Answers
1 truth 2 colt 3 niece 4 they 5 wild 6 vague 7 field
8 most 9 haste 10 guy 11 both 12 lose 13 view
14 feud 15 wound 16 brief 17 shriek 18 rogue
19 thieves 20 guide 21 beige 22 mild 23 grieve

24 yield   25 plague   26 move   27 height   28 wield
29 stroll   30 grief   31 youth   32 group   33 rouge
34 siege   35 though   36 taste

Skill Drill 23 Answers
1 who   2 vein   3 prey   4 rein   5 break   6 buy   7 prove
8 soul   9 you   10 soup   11 weigh   12 great   13 through
14 roll   15 shoe   16 hey   17 steak   18 bass   19 neigh
20 piece   21 whose   22 route   23 poll   24 waste
25 whom   26 dough

Skill Drill 24 Answers
1 put   2 could   3 bush   4 wolf   5 should   6 bull   7 push
8 wolves   9 full

Skill Drill 25 Answers
1 guard, heart   2 bear, wear

Skill Drill 26 Answers
1 Four, court   2 worms, worth

Skill Drill 27 Answers
1 hearth   2 work   3 floor   4 yearn   5 source   6 earth
7 where   8 court   9 learn   10 were   11 word   12 worth
13 worse   14 scourge

Skill Drill 28 Answers
1 are   2 heard   3 tear   4 four   5 course   6 earn   7 heir
8 there   9 wear

Answers for Chapter 2 Additional Skill Drills

Additional Skill Drill 1 Answers
1 wreath   2 ghost   3 wrench   4 badge   5 gnaw   6 knife
7 knight   8 thigh   9 palm   10 crutch   11 thumb   12 calves
13 scratch   14 judge   15 gnome   16 knot

Additional Skill Drill 2 Answers

1 laugh 2 one 3 bread 4 wash 5 sieve 6 swan
7 cough 8 yacht

Additional Skill Drill 3 Answers

1 eye 2 post 3 ski 4 weight 5 veil 6 move 7 sleigh
8 gauge 9 paste 10 child 11 sew 12 scroll 13 pint
14 shield 15 freight 16 ninth

Additional Skill Drill 4 Answers

1 door 2 pearl 3 fourth 4 heart 5 bear 6 worm
7 pour 8 pear 9 guard 10 four 11 floor 12 sour
13 court 14 roar 15 hair 16 star 17 earth 18 burst
19 scarf 20 burn 21 there 22 wear 23 work 24 learn

3 The Tricky Homonyms

A homonym is a word that has the same pronunciation as another word but has a different meaning and spelling. There are over 2,000 homonym groups in English. You have met many of these homonym word groups in your spelling lessons. This chapter reviews one-syllable homonyms.

The homonym spellings follow the same patterns as do other one-syllable words. Some homonym word groups have regular or expected spellings. Some groups have a snurk spelling, and a few have only snurk spellings. The snurks in the review lists are marked by the snurk symbol (▽).

Remember which meaning goes with each homonym spelling. The review lists remind you of the homonym meanings by using them in sentences or phrases or by defining them.

Short-Vowel Homonyms

Some homonym groups have expected short-vowel spellings although they may have silent or doubled consonants. Read the homonyms and use the correct one in each of the sentences.

rap to *rap* on the door
wrap to *wrap* a package
1 Jerry is about to __ a present.

sell to *sell* candy

cell a small room; a small unit of living matter

2 This is a prison __.

rest to *rest* in bed

wrest to twist or pull

3 Maria is trying to __ it away.

sent past tense of *send*

cent a penny

scent a nice smell

4 What a lovely __!

ring anything round

wring to squeeze hard

5 Carlos can __ a lot of water out of that garment.

in *in* the house

inn a restaurant or tavern

6 She's about to go into the __.

its *its* fur is soft

it's it is

7 __ getting pretty late.

him We like *him.*

hymn a song of praise

8 They're singing a __.

not He is *not* here.

knot to tie a *knot*

9 That is a big __!

rung a step on a ladder
wrung past tense of *wring*
10 The __ on this ladder are broken.

plum a fruit
plumb a weight on a line
11 She's using a __ line.

Check your answers for the sentences on page 83.

B Short-Vowel Homonyms with Snurks

Read the pairs of homonyms. Write the correct one for each missing word.

ant an insect
▽ *aunt*[1] a relative
1 __ Martha doesn't like __.

red the color
▽ *read*[2] past tense of *read* /rēd/
2 She must have __ the book.

led past tense of *lead* /lēd/
▽ *lead*[3] a metal
3 That's a lot of __!

bred past tense of *breed*
▽ *bread* a loaf of *bread*
4 That's not __! It's __.

[1]When pronounced /ônt/, *aunt* is not a homonym.
[2]When pronounced /rēd/, *read* is not a homonym for *red.*
[3]When pronounced /lēd/, *lead* is not a homonym.

bin a storage place

▽ *been* He has *been* here.

5 Never get caught in a coal __.

gilt gold paint

▽ *guilt* blame for wrongdoing

6 No doubt about his __!

sun the *sun* is shining

▽ *son* his mother's *son*

7 She's showing the __ to her __.

nun a religious sister

▽ *none* not any

8 She will have __ of that.

ruff a collar

▽ *rough* not smooth

9 Her __ must be very __!

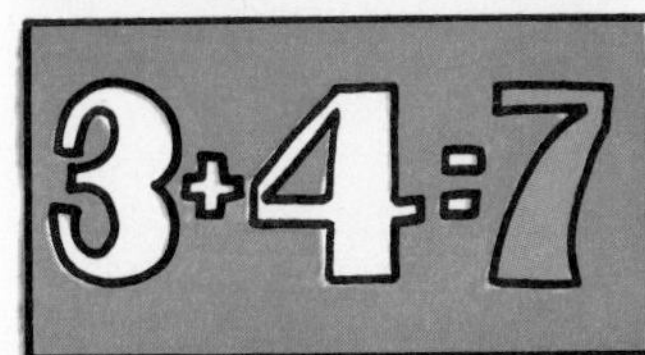

sum amount

▽ *some* a few

10 That's the __.

▽ *one* 1

▽ *won* past tense of *win*

11 He must have __ the race.

Check your answers for the sentences in Section B on page 83.

Skill Drill 1 Write the homonyms for the sound-spellings. Beside each sound-spelling is a clue for which word to write first.

1 /led/ (a metal)
2 /him/ (a song)
3 /in/ (a restaurant)
4 /rap/ (to tie up)
5 /sel/ (a small room)
6 /sum/ (a few)
7 /bin/ (a storage place)
8 /rest/ (to pull away)
9 /its/ (a contraction for "it is")
10 /rung/ (a step on a ladder)
11 /gilt/ (a kind of paint)
12 /plum/ (a kind of fruit)

Long-Vowel Homonyms

Many of these long-vowel homonyms have regular or expected spellings.

made past tense of *make*
maid a girl; a female servant
1 A pretty ___!

male a man or boy
mail You *mail* a letter.
2 She's delivering the ___.

pane a sheet of glass
pain a hurt
3 He must be in ___.

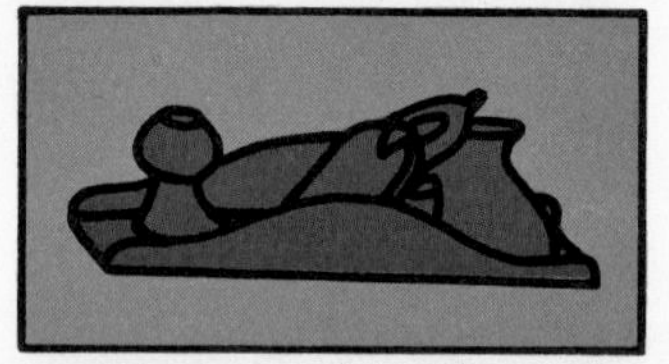

plane an airplane; a carpenter's tool
plain clear; not fancy; level land
4 This is just a ___ old ___.

sale the act of selling
sail a cloth on a ship to catch wind
5 What a ___!

tale a story
tail a part of an animal's body
6 She's reading a ___.

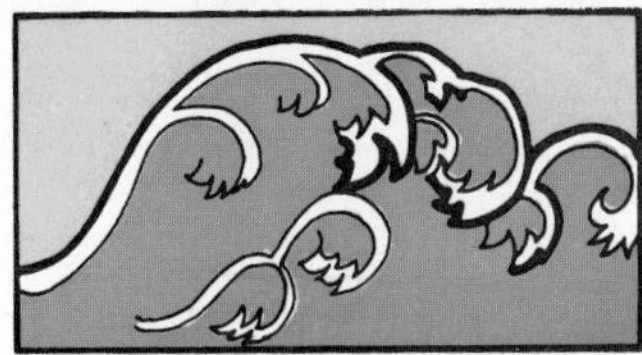

wave a moving swell of water
waive to give up
7 Those are big ___!

gate a door in a fence
gait a manner of walking or running
8 This is a ___, not a ___.

bale a large bundle
bail money to set a person free
9 That's a ___ of hay.

pale without much color
pail bucket
10 That's not a very good ___.

ale beer
ail to feel sick
11 Something must ___ him.

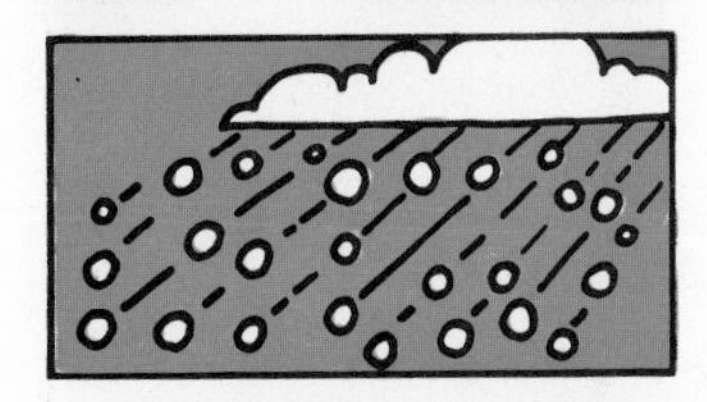

hale strong and healthy
hail round pieces of falling ice; to greet or shout at
12 That's some ___!

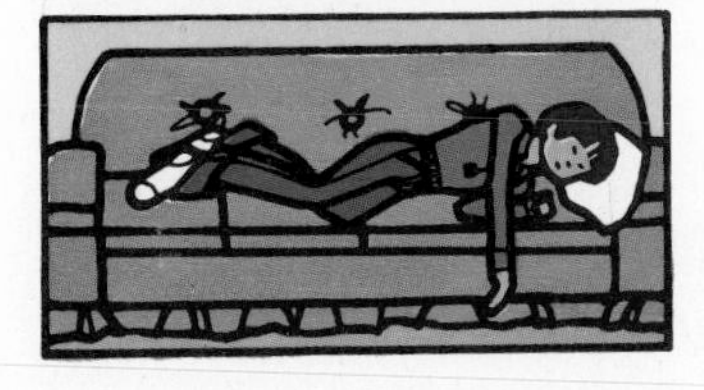

lane a narrow road
lain He had *lain* down.
13 He has ___ down to rest.

mane hair on the neck of a horse or lion
main most important; a large pipe
14 Did you ever see such a big __?

maze a network of paths
maize corn
15 You can call it corn or __.

raze to tear down
raise to lift; an increase in pay
16 They're going to __ this building.

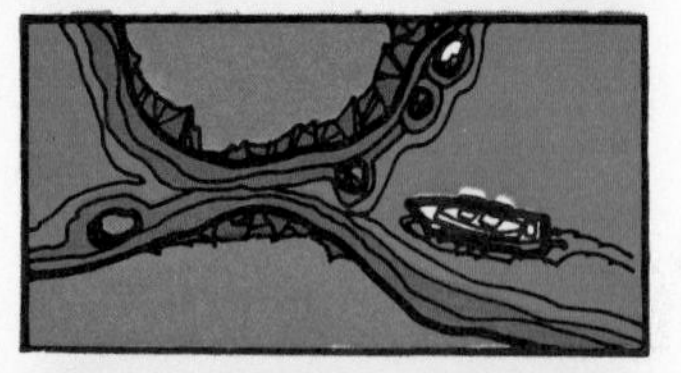

straight without a bend
strait a channel connecting two bodies of water
17 This is how a __ looks to a pilot.

feet plural of *foot*
feat a great deed
18 Charles performed quite a __!

cheep a young bird's cry
cheap costing little
19 She's saying, "__! __!"

need to be in want of
knead to press and squeeze dough
20 You might say she __ to __ dough.

teem to be full of
team a basketball *team*
21 The players on this __ are short.

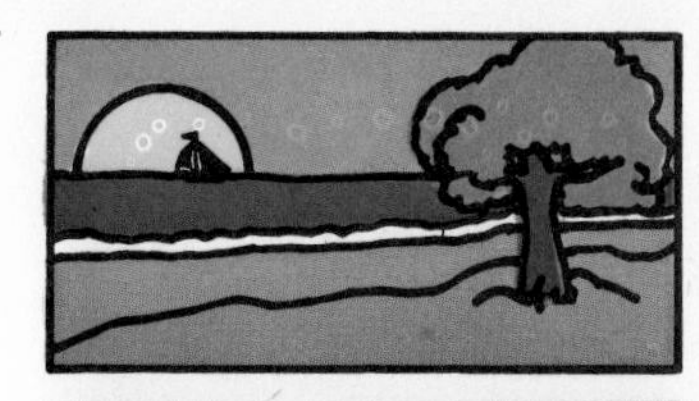

beech a tree
beach a flat shore of sand
22 Ah, a __ tree on a __!

meet to come together
meat animal flesh
23 __ the man who sells __.

reed tall grass
read[4] to *read* a book
24 She got into some tall __.

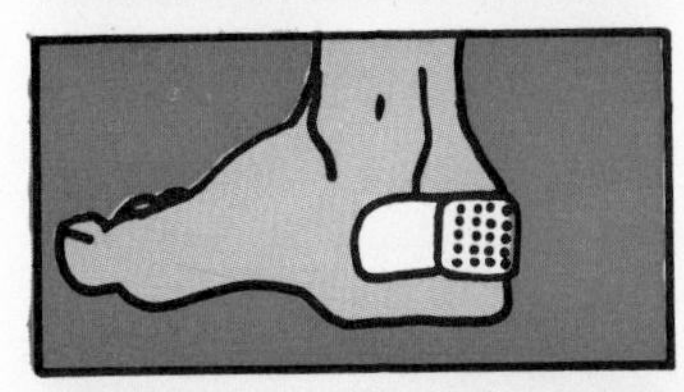

heel the *heel* on a shoe
heal to make well
25 We hope her __ will __ soon.

bee an insect
be He will *be* here.
26 This must be a __.

beet a plant
beat to hit; to overcome
27 You can't __ the price of these __.

flee to run away
flea an insect
28 He must have a __.

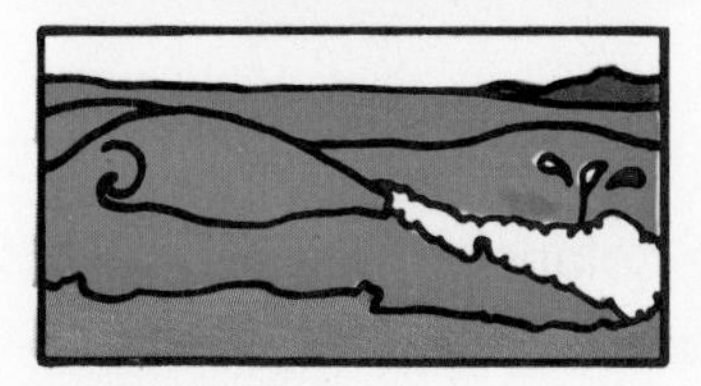

see to look at
sea a large body of water
29 You can __ a __ here.

[4]When pronounced /red/, *read* is not a homonym for *reed*.

seen We have *seen* you.
scene a view; a picture; a part of a play
30 A lovely __!

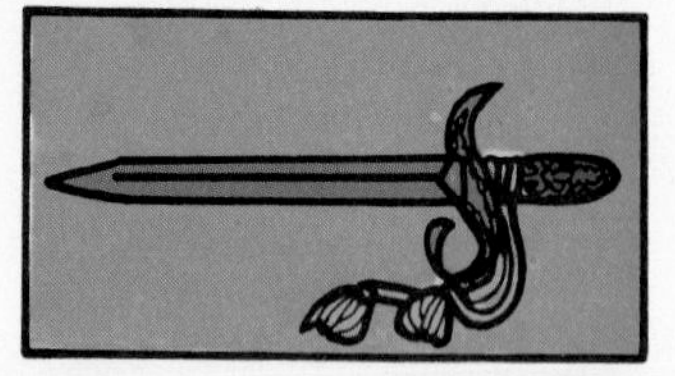

steel the metal
steal to take dishonestly
31 It must be made of __.

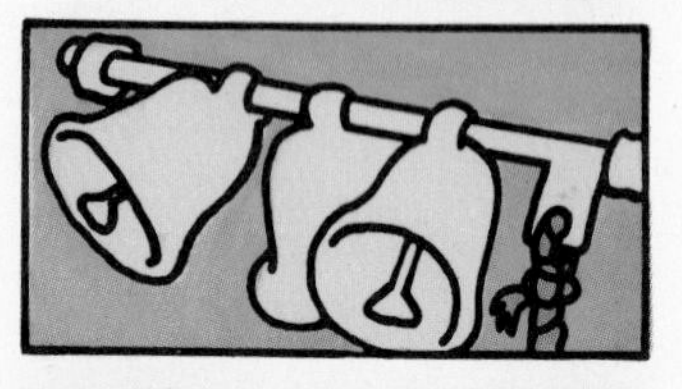

peal the ringing of bells
peel to strip the skin from
32 The bells are __.

week seven days
weak not strong
33 He must be __!

night the time from sunset to sunrise
knight a warrior in armor
34 A noble __!

rite a solemn ceremony
right *right* hand; *right* way
write to *write* with a pen
35 He's performing a __.

tide the rise and fall of the ocean
tied the past tense of *tie*
36 It must be high __.

die to stop living
dye coloring matter; to use coloring matter
37 She's going to __ the cloth.

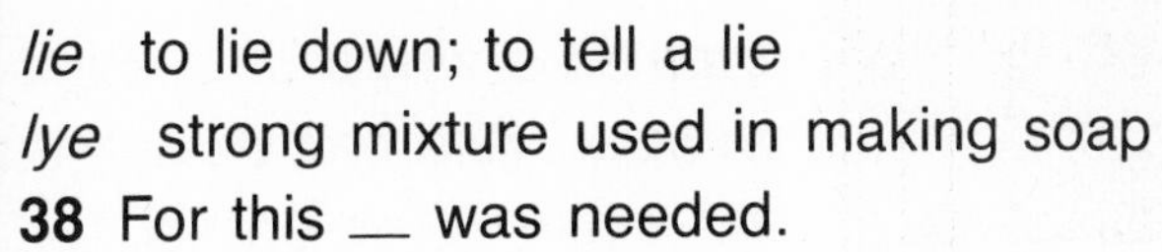

lie to lie down; to tell a lie
lye strong mixture used in making soap
38 For this __ was needed.

site a position or place; a building *site*
cite to quote; to *cite* the law
sight the power of seeing
39 She's about to __ the law.

stile the steps for getting over a fence
style fashion; a way of doing things
40 She's leaping over the __ in fine __.

no I have *no* pencil.
know We *know* our lesson.
41 You __ he's saying, "__!"

rode the past tense of *ride*
road a way between places
42 Kim __ down the __.

lone without others
loan anything lent, like money
43 He's a __ wolf.

groan to make a sound of pain
grown She has *grown* up.
44 This __ man is __.

shone the past tense of *shine*
shown We were *shown* how to drive.
45 The sun must have __ on him.

throne a king's or queen's chair
thrown She has *thrown* the ball.
46 She's sitting on her __.

toe the *toe* of a foot
tow to pull by rope or chain
47 They had to __ it.

blew the past tense of *blow*
blue a color
48 The paint is __.

new not old
knew the past tense of *know*
49 That's not a __ baby!

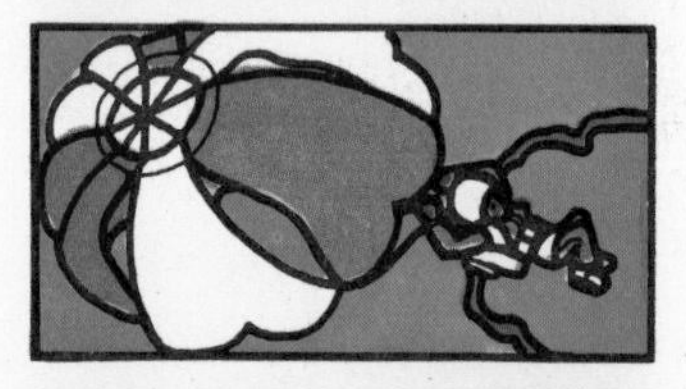

shoot to *shoot* a gun
chute a parachute
50 Her __ is open.

flew the past tense of *fly*
flue a pipe for letting out smoke
51 The fly __ up the __.

hue color
hew to cut or chop
52 He's going to __ it down.

Check your answers for the sentences in Section C on page 83.

Skill Drill 2 Read the twenty meanings below. There are homonyms for each of them. Review all of the long-vowel homonyms in Section C beginning on page 60. Write the homonyms for the meanings. Be sure to check your answers with those at the end of this chapter.

1 ice pellets
2 healthy
3 corn
4 puzzle
5 animal flesh
6 come together
7 run away
8 an insect
9 stop living
10 change color
11 past tense of *fly*
12 air vent
13 past tense of *know*
14 not old
15 ceremony
16 make letters
17 correct
18 power of seeing
19 quote
20 place

Skill Drill 3 Write the homonyms for the sound-spellings. Beside each sound-spelling is a clue for which word to write first. Write first the homonym for the meaning that is given. Then write the other homonyms for the sound-spellings. Be sure to check your answers.

1 /wāv/ (to give up)
2 /strāt/ (no curve)
3 /bē/ (an insect)
4 /lī/ (untruth)
5 /lōn/ (single)
6 /stēl/ (a metal)
7 /shōn/ (the past tense of *shine*)
8 /shüt/ (a parachute)
9 /lān/ (narrow road)
10 /tēm/ (a group of players)
11 /bēt/ (to hit)
12 /nō/ (to understand)
13 /sēn/ (the past tense of *see*)
14 /grōn/ (to cry out)
15 /blü/ (a color)

Long-Vowel Homonyms with Snurks

Some of the long-vowel homonyms include snurks. Here are some that do.

pray to *pray* in church
▽ *prey* a hunted animal
1 He's about to seize his __.

way to find your *way*
▽ *weigh* to *weigh* on a scale
2 He shouldn't __ himself now!

wait to *wait* for a bus
▽ *weight* how heavy a thing is; a lead *weight*
3 That's not much __.

waist a belt around your *waist*
▽ *waste* to spend uselessly; leftover material
4 Here is a new __ can.

vale a valley
▽ *veil* something that screens or hides
5 She's wearing a __.

vane a weather *vane*
vain too proud of oneself; of no use
▽ *vein* a blood tube
6 This one is a __.

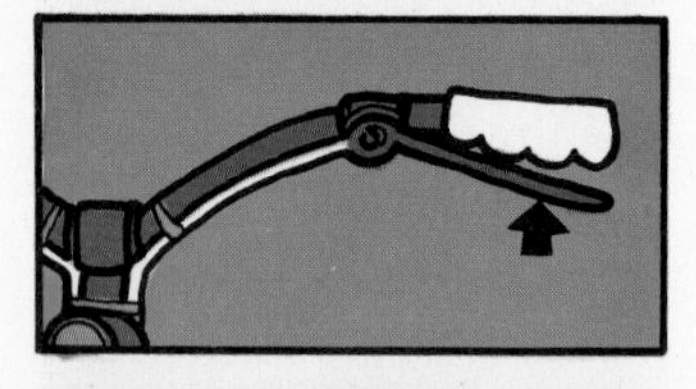

brake a stopper
▽ *break* to come apart
7 This is a __, not a __.

grate an iron framework
▽ *great* big; important
8 He was a __ man.

rain the water from clouds
▽ *rein* a strap to guide animals
▽ *reign* to rule
9 His business is to __.

slay to kill
▽ *sleigh* a sled
10 It's fun to ride in an old-fashioned __.

nay no
▽ *neigh* a sound made by horses
11 Only a horse can __.

stake a tent *stake*
▽ *steak* meat
12 You can't eat this __.

base bottom; a baseball *base*
▽ *bass* a low sound
13 That is a big __ drum.

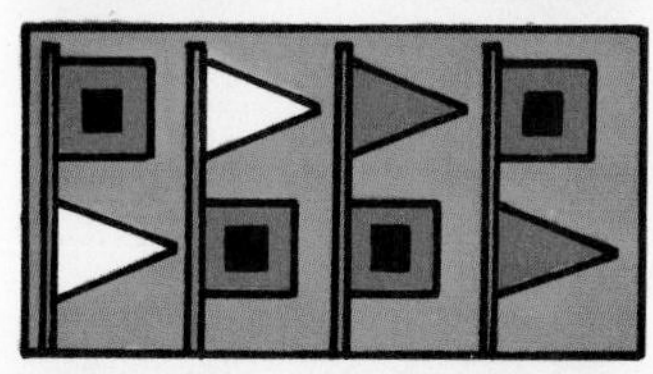

ate the past tense of *eat*
▽ *eight* a number
14 Here are __ flags.

peace quiet; no war
▽ *piece* a part, a *piece* of pie
15 This is a sign of __.

I'll I will
▽ *isle* a small island
▽ *aisle* a passage between rows
16 This is not much of an __.

I a person
▽ *eye* an organ of sight
▽ *aye* yes
17 They're saying "__."

by to stop *by*
▽ *buy* to *buy* at a store
18 They want to __.

quire 24 sheets of paper
▽ *choir* a singing group
19 This group is a __.

role actor's part
▽ *roll* to turn over; a list of names
20 He's calling the __.

pole a *pole* for a flag
▽ *poll* a place for voting
21 They're casting votes at the __.

hole an opening
▽ *whole* all; complete; in one piece
22 She's looking into a __.

sole only; bottom of a foot; a fish
▽ *soul* spirit
23 This is a __, not a __.

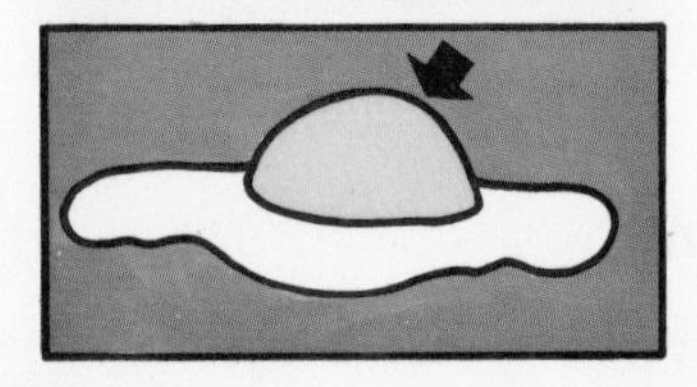

yoke a harness frame; upper part of a dress
▽ *yolk* the yellow part of an egg
24 This part is a __.

doe a female deer, goat, or rabbit
▽ *dough* *dough* to make bread
25 She's a ___.

due to be returned
dew *dew* on flowers
▽ *do* *Do* your work.
26 Her payment is ___.

threw the past tense of *throw*
▽ *through* to go *through* the doorway
27 Jennifer ___ it.

too also
▽ *two* 2
▽ *to* go *to* school
28 You see ___ *too*'s.

yew an evergreen tree
▽ *you* the person spoken to
▽ *ewe* a female sheep
29 This is a ___ under the ___.

root the plant part below ground
▽ *route*[5] a way to go

Skill Drill 4 Write the correct homonyms to complete the sentences. Check your answers.

1 Our flag hangs on a /pōl/ ___.
2 The catcher threw to second /bās/ ___.
3 Dominick drove a /stāk/ ___ into the ground.
4 Our library books are /dü/ ___ today.
5 Mark the /rüt/ ___ on the map.
6 Olga tied a sash around her /wāst/ ___.

[5]When pronounced /rout/, *route* is not a homonym for *root.*

Two-Vowel and Vowel-*r* Homonyms

Write the correct homonym for each missing word.

bough a tree branch
bow[6] to bend; front of a ship
1 This is a __.

our belonging to us
hour 60 minutes
2 The __ is one o'clock.

rout a complete defeat; to dig out
route[7] a way to go
3 Are we on the right __?

fowl a bird
foul dirty; not fair; to tangle
4 This __ uses __ language!

hall a passage: a large room
haul to pull or drag; to transport
5 They __ heavy loads.

cord a thick string; a measure of wood
chord two or more music notes combined
6 This one is a __.

sore painful
soar to fly high; to rise
7 It __ high in the sky.

[6]When pronounced /bō/, *bow* is not a homonym.
[7]When pronounced /rüt/, *route* is not a homonym for *rout.*

oar a pole with flat end
ore rock containing metal
8 He's looking for __.

pore to study; a small opening
▽ *pour* to flow
9 She's __ over her book.

horse an animal
hoarse sounding rough
10 She will be __.

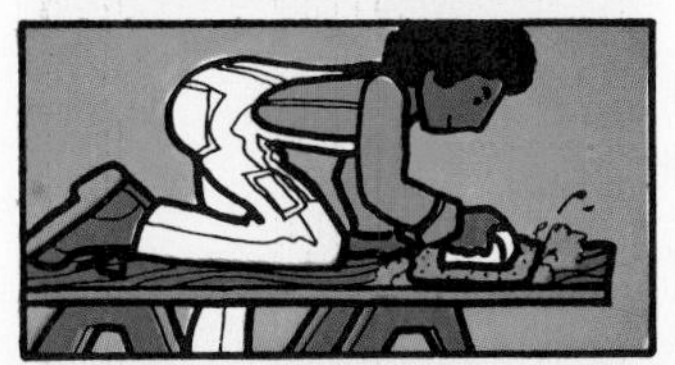

coarse rough; not fine; vulgar
▽ *course* a path, track; series of lessons; part of a meal; golf *course;* of *course*
11 Of __ it's __!

hoard to save and store
horde a crowd
12 That's a __ of people!

board a flat piece of wood; meals for pay; get on
bored made weary; made a hole with a sharp tool
13 Richard must be __.

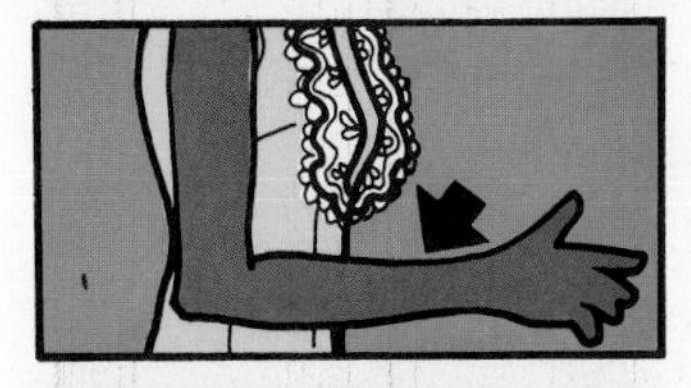

for a present *for* you
fore the front part
▽ *four* 4
14 That's the __ part of her arm.

core the central part
▽ *corps* a group of soldiers
15 The __ is marching.

forth forward; he came *forth*
▽ *fourth* , 4th
16 She hopes the mouse will come __.

fir a tree
fur a *fur* coat
17 This must be a __ tree.

berth a place to sleep
birth coming into life
18 He's in the upper __.

urn a vase with a foot; coffeepot
▽ *earn* to be paid for work
19 And this is an __.

fair just; average; light; sunny
fare money for riding
20 She's collecting the __.

bare naked
▽ *bear* an animal; to carry; to put up with
21 This __ has __ feet.

stare to look long and hard
stair a series of steps
22 He is __.

ware pottery
▽ *wear* to have on the body
23 He's __ a new suit.

air the *air* you breathe
▽ *heir* a person with right to someone's property after his death
24 The younger one is the __.

hare a large rabbit
hair *hair* on your head
25 Now here's a head of __!

flare to flame up; a brief light; to spread out
flair a natural talent
26 He has a __ for music.

▽ *there* over *there*
▽ *their* belonging to them
▽ *they're* they are
27 __ off!

pair two
pare to peel
▽ *pear* a fruit
28 He's __ the __.

peer an equal; to look closely
▽ *pier* a landing place for boats
29 She's __ at the __.

dear a *dear* friend
deer an animal
30 This is a __.

sheer very thin; unmixed; steep; to swerve
shear to cut with shears
31 She's __ the __ cloth.

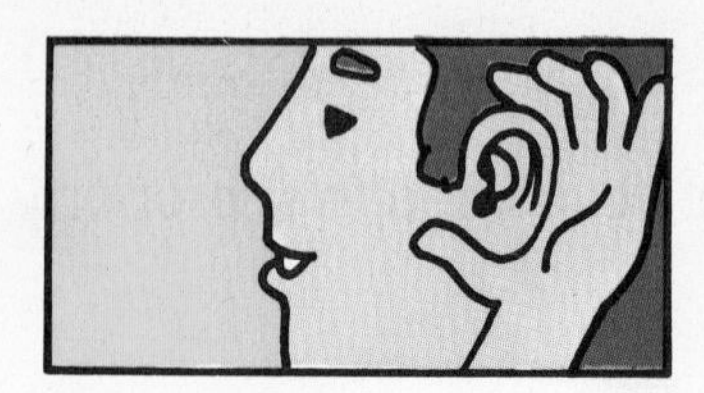

hear to take in sounds
∇ *here* at this place
32 He can't __ very well.

Skill Drill 5 Write the correct homonyms to complete the sentences. Check your answers.

1 We wear clothes, but we sell /wãrz/ __.
2 Misers never get /bôrd/ __ with their /hôrdz/ __ of gold.
3 A wealthy /ãr/ __ need not /ėrn/ __ money.
4 A vase on the steps is like an /ėrn/ __ on the /stãrz/ __.
5 The new /ãr/ __ /rout/ __ will take one /our/ __ to fly.
6 "Quadruplets!" he cried, as the /fôrth/ __ /bėrth/ __ was announced.
7 /our/ __ /dir/ __ friend slept in the upper /bėrth/ __.
8 We could /hir/ __ him play /kôrdz/ __ out in the /hôl/ __.
9 It is /shir/ __ joy to watch the eagle /sôr/ __.
10 The old mine is full of /ôr/ __.
11 Don't eat the /kôr/ __ of the apple.
12 Helena's /hãr/ __ was neatly combed.

Summary

Homonyms are words like *their* and *there* that have the same pronunciation but different spellings and different meanings. In this chapter you have reviewed 136 one-syllable homonym word groups that you will probably need when you write. You can learn the spellings of these homonyms just as you learn the spellings of other one-syllable words: by noting expected spellings, silent-letter patterns, and unexpected, or snurk, spellings. Remember which spelling goes with each meaning.

Mastery Test 3

A

Write the sentences. Spell the words correctly.

1 She /tīd/ ___ /fôr/ ___ /nots/ ___ /in/ ___ /wun/ ___ /pēs/ ___ of /kôrs/ ___ /kôrd/ ___.

2 My /dir/ ___ /ant/ ___ bought /tü/ ___ /chēp/ ___ /ringz/ ___ on /sāl/ ___ last /wēk/ ___.

3 /ī/ ___ /nēd/ ___ /āt/ ___ egg /yōks/ ___ in this /bred/ ___ /dō/ ___ before I can /nēd/ ___ it.

4 Those in the /ãr/ ___ /kôr/ ___ /ėrn/ ___ /fãr/ ___ wages /fôr/ ___ /ŦHãr/ ___ work.

5 /hôl/ ___ these /led/ ___ pipes /tü/ ___ the /pir/ ___ and /wāt/ ___ to have them /wād/ ___.

6 /sum/ ___ /gilt/ ___ paint on the /pōl/ ___ /bī/ ___ the /gāt/ ___ has /pēld/ ___ in the /sun/ ___.

7 "/plān/ ___ /red/ ___ and /blü/ ___ /vālz/ ___ are /not/ ___ in /stīl/ ___," cried the /mād/ ___.

8 A /pãr/ ___ of /hãrz/ ___ /pird/ ___ at a /dō/ ___ and /dir/ ___ from a /hōl/ ___ under the /fėr/ ___ tree.

9 What /mād/ ___ the /bou/ ___ of that tree /brāk/ ___?

10 /dü/ ___ /ū/ ___ /sē/ ___ that /lōn/ ___ /ū/ ___ in the /ūz/ ___ to the /rīt/ ___ of the /rōd/ ___?

11 The /fôrth/ ___ man from the /īl/ ___ is the /bās/ ___ voice when /our/ ___ /kwīr/ ___ sings /himz/ ___.

12 /sôrz/ ___ on his /tōz/ ___, /hēlz/ ___, and /sōlz/ ___ of his /fēt/ ___ /mād/ ___ /him/ ___ /grōn/ ___ with /pān/ ___.

13 Wind /blü/ ___ for /ourz/ ___ and /rān/ ___ /pôrd/ ___ /thrü/ ___ the window /pān/ ___.

14 We /bēt/ ___ the /rest/ ___ of the /tēmz/ ___ and /wun/ ___ the /mēt/ ___ without /wun/ ___ /ruf/ ___ play.

15 We'll /sāl/ ___ across the /strāt/ ___ to an /īl/ ___ in the /sē/ ___ and live /ŦHãr/ ___ till we /dī/ ___.

16 He /bôrd/ ___ everyone with /tālz/ ___ of /foul/ ___ deeds by /hôrdz/ ___ of outlaws.

B

Write the missing homonyms for these phrases.

1 a well-/bred/ __ horse
2 /bī/ __ and /sel/ __ goods
3 the /sent/ __ of roses
4 a /bin/ __ of corn
5 admit his /gilt/ __
6 /bēt/ __ of a drum
7 the horse's /gāt/ __
8 a drink of /āl/ __
9 /tō/ __ the barge
10 birds of /prā/ __
11 the /ãr/ __ to the /thrōn/ __
12 a /kwīr/ __ of paper
13 a wooden /bôrd/ __
14 fill the /ėrn/ __
15 a soft /bėrth/ __
16 a /red/ __ /plum/ __
17 a /yōk/ __ of oxen
18 a weather /vān/ __
19 /wāv/ __ your hand
20 /flē/ __ from the storm
21 /stēl/ __ the gold
22 a /māz/ __ of paths
23 a /bāl/ __ of cotton
24 /ring/ __ the wet cloth
25 a /grōn/ __ dog
26 a /wāst/ __ of time
27 /ôr/ __ from the mine
28 /fãr/ __ balls and /foul/ __ balls
29 the lion's /mān/ __
30 the /rüt/ __ of a plant
31 /pôr/ __ the milk

Additional Skill Drills

Do these skill drills if you want to improve your Mastery Test score.

Additional Skill Drill 1 Write the picture words. Below each word, write the homonym. Check your answers at the end of Chapter 3.

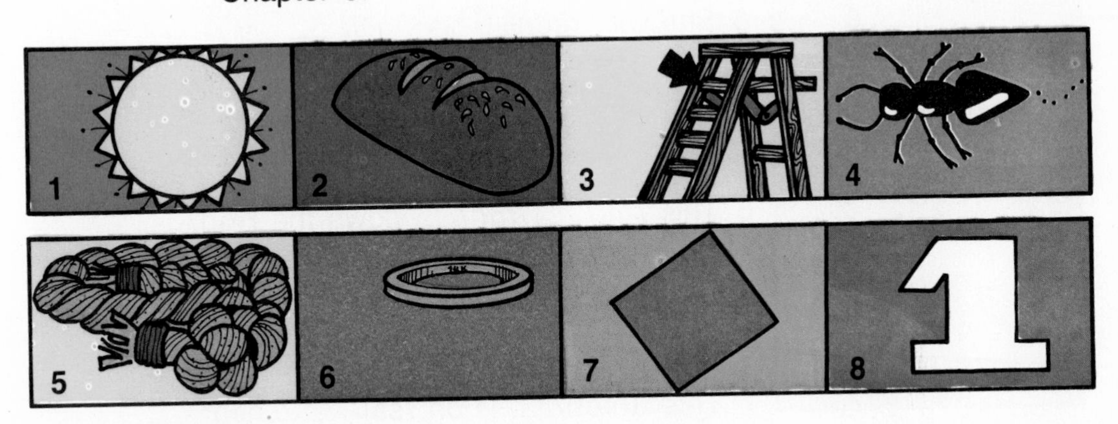

Additional Skill Drill 2 Write the long-vowel homonyms for these sentences. Check your answers.

1 Sue will /hū/ __ down that /bēch/ __ tree.

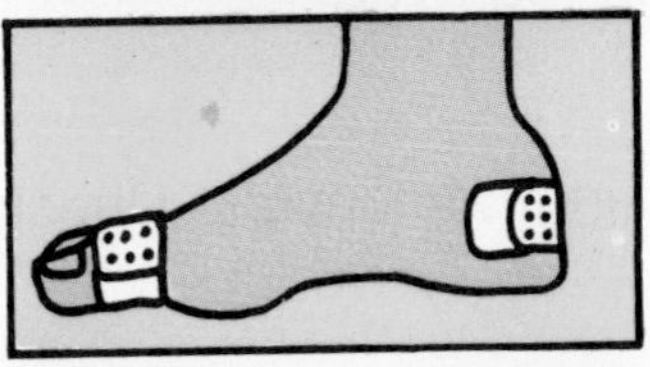

2 His /tō/ __ and /hēl/ __ hurt.

3 Only the /māl/ __ lion has a /mān/ __.

4 He got his /tāl/ __ caught in the /gāt/ __.

5 She will /rēd/ __ his /māl/ __.

6 This /nīt/ __ /rōd/ __ down the /rōd/ __.

7 This /thrōn/ __ is on /sāl/ __ /chēp/ __.

8 He is too /wēk/ __ to /rāz/ __ the /bāl/ __.

9 You can /sē/ __ the /plān/ __ fly over the /plān/ __.
10 Joe has /pān/ __ in his /fēt/ __.
11 One /mād/ __ carried a /pāl/ __ of milk over the /stīl/ __.
12 The /sē/ __ covers the /bēch/ __ at high /tīd/ __.

Additional Skill Drill 3 Write the missing homonyms. Check your answers.

1 Carmen /thrü/ __ the ball /thrü/ __ the /hōl/ __.

2 She wants /tü/ __ /bī/ __ that /hōl/ __ /pēs/ __ of /stāk/ __.

3 He'll /yōk/ __ the /dō/ __ to the /slā/ __.

4 The /rützˈ/ __ on this /ū/ __ tree were /tü/ __ short.

5 The /wāt/ __ of the /prā/ __ is /tü/ __ /grāt/ __.

6 /pēs/ __ /rānz/ __ on this /īl/ __.

7 They /dü/ __ make those /bās/ __ drums /rōl/ __.

8 He must /wāt/ __ to /wā/ __ his /dō/ __.

9 The Reds beat /bī/ __ a score of /āt/ __ /tü/ __ /tü/ __.
10 The /pōl/ __ shows more /ī/ __ votes than /nā/ __ votes.
11 His /rōl/ __ is to lead the /wā/ __ down the /īl/ __ for the /kwīr/ __.

Additional Skill Drill 4 Write the right homonyms. Check your answers.

1 Becky is steering a /kôrs/ ___ with an /ôr/ ___ in the /bou/ ___ or /fôr/ ___ part of the canoe.

2 The Scout /kôr/ ___ is being put to /rout/ ___ by a /hôrd/ ___ of angry bees.

3 This /hãr/ ___ has a /flãr/ ___ /fôr/ ___ leaping over /flãrz/ ___!

4 /ŦHãr/ ___ being told to pay /ŦHãr/ ___ /fãr/ ___ over /ŦHãr/ ___.

5 With that /sôr/ ___ throat, her voice must be /hôrs/ ___.

6 One will /pir/ ___ and one will /stãr/ ___. Will the ball go /foul/ ___ or /fãr/ ___?

7 /fôr/ ___ /foul/ ___ are perched on the /bãr/ ___ /bou/ ___ of a /fėr/ ___ tree.

8 This /hôrs/ ___ can hardly /hôl/ ___ this /kôrd/ ___ of wooden /bôrdz/ ___.

Answers for Chapter 3 Skill Drills

Answers for Sentences in Section A

1 wrap 2 cell 3 wrest 4 scent 5 wring 6 inn 7 It's 8 hymn 9 knot 10 rungs 11 plumb

Answers for Sentences in Section B

1 Aunt, ants 2 read 3 lead 4 bred, bread 5 bin 6 guilt 7 sun, son 8 none 9 ruff, rough 10 sum 11 won

Skill Drill 1 Answers

1 lead, led 2 hymn, him 3 inn, in 4 wrap, rap 5 cell, sell 6 some, sum 7 bin, been 8 wrest, rest 9 it's, its 10 rung, wrung 11 gilt, guilt 12 plum, plumb

Answers for Sentences in Section C

1 maid 2 mail 3 pain 4 plain, plane 5 sale 6 tale 7 waves 8 gate, gait 9 bale 10 pail 11 ail 12 hail 13 lain 14 mane 15 maize 16 raze 17 strait 18 feat 19 Cheep! Cheep! 20 needs, knead 21 team 22 beech, beach 23 Meet, meat 24 reeds 25 heel, heal 26 bee 27 beat, beets 28 flea 29 see, sea 30 scene 31 steel 32 pealing 33 weak 34 knight 35 rite 36 tide 37 dye 38 lye 39 cite 40 stile, style 41 know, No 42 rode, road 43 lone 44 grown, groaning 45 shone 46 throne 47 tow 48 blue 49 new 50 chute 51 flew, flue 52 hew

Skill Drill 2 Answers

1 hail 2 hale 3 maize 4 maze 5 meat 6 meet 7 flee 8 flea 9 die 10 dye 11 flew 12 flue 13 knew 14 new 15 rite 16 write 17 right 18 sight 19 cite 20 site

Skill Drill 3 Answers

1 waive, wave 2 straight, strait 3 bee, be 4 lie, lye 5 lone, loan 6 steel, steal 7 shone, shown 8 chute, shoot 9 lane, lain 10 team, teem 11 beat, beet 12 know, no 13 seen, scene 14 groan, grown 15 blue, blew

Answers for Sentences in Section D

1 prey 2 weigh 3 weight 4 waste 5 veil 6 vane
7 brake, break 8 great 9 reign 10 sleigh 11 neigh
12 stake 13 bass 14 eight 15 peace 16 isle 17 aye
18 buy 19 choir 20 roll 21 poll 22 hole 23 sole, soul
24 yolk 25 doe 26 due 27 threw 28 two 29 ewe, yew

Skill Drill 4 Answers

1 pole 2 base 3 stake 4 due 5 route 6 waist

Answers for Sentences in Section E

1 bough 2 hour 3 route 4 fowl, foul 5 haul 6 chord
7 soars 8 ore 9 poring 10 hoarse 11 course, coarse
12 horde 13 bored 14 fore 15 corps 16 forth 17 fir
18 berth 19 urn 20 fare 21 bear, bare 22 staring
23 wearing 24 heir 25 hair 26 flair 27 They're
28 paring, pears 29 peering, pier 30 deer 31 shearing, sheer 32 hear

Skill Drill 5 Answers

1 wares 2 bored, hoards 3 heir, earn 4 urn, stairs
5 air, route, hour 6 fourth, birth 7 Our, dear, berth
8 hear, chords, hall 9 sheer, soar 10 ore 11 core
12 hair

Answers for Chapter 3 Additional Skill Drills

Additional Skill Drill 1 Answers

1 sun, son 2 bread, bred 3 rung, wrung 4 ant, aunt
5 knot, not 6 ring, wring 7 red, read 8 one, won

Additional Skill Drill 2 Answers

1 hew, beech 2 toe, heel 3 male, mane 4 tail, gate
5 read, mail 6 knight, rode, road 7 throne, sale, cheap
8 weak, raise, bale 9 see, plane, plain 10 pain, feet
11 maid, pail, stile 12 sea, beach, tide

Additional Skill Drill 3 Answers

1 threw, through, hole 2 to, buy, whole, piece, steak 3 yoke, doe, sleigh 4 roots, yew, too 5 weight, prey, too, great 6 Peace, reigns, isle 7 do, bass, roll 8 wait, weigh, dough 9 by, eight, to, two 10 poll, aye, nay 11 role, way, aisle, choir

Additional Skill Drill 4 Answers

1 course, oar, bow, fore 2 corps, rout, horde 3 hare, flair, for, flares 4 They're, their, fare, there 5 sore, hoarse 6 peer, stare, foul, fair 7 Four, fowl, bare, bough, fir 8 horse, haul, cord, boards

4 Compounds

A compound word is a word made up of two or more smaller words. Compound words are no harder to spell than the small words used to form them. You need to *see* the little words that make up the compound word. In this chapter the compound word parts will be marked to remind you to look at them rather than to see one long word. We call these marked parts the *eye-syllables.*

When you *say* long words, you say them by parts, or syllables. The dictionary shows the very short stops between spoken syllables by a space between them. We call these separated word parts in the sound-spellings the *ear-syllables.*

eye-syllables	ear-syllables
base ball	/bās bôl/
	syllable space

When we say two-syllable compound words, we usually say one syllable louder than the other syllable. In most compounds, though, we say the softer syllable loud enough to hear its vowel sound clearly. The dictionary shows the louder syllable with a heavy *accent,* or *stress* mark, and the softer syllable with a lighter accent, or stress mark. The heavier mark is the *primary* accent mark, and the lighter one is the *secondary* accent mark.

primary accent mark — secondary accent mark

/bās′ bôl′/

Chapter 1 reviewed the spelling options for four basic groups of one-syllable words: (1) short-vowel words, (2) long-vowel words, (3) two-letter vowel words, (4) vowel-*r* words. *The parts of compound words have the same spelling options.* Spell the compound word parts the same way as the one-syllable words.

Short-Vowel Compounds

The short-vowel sounds in compound eye-syllables are spelled with *a, e, i, o,* and *u.*

a spells /a/ grand stand
e spells /e/ them selves
i spells /i/ lip stick
o spells /o/ top notch
u spells /u/ hum drum

Some compounds have different short-vowel spellings in each of the eye-syllables.

/a/ /o/	/u/ /e/	/i/ /e/
padlock	sunset	indent

Long-Vowel Compounds

The long-vowel spellings appear in compounds.

Vowel Sounds	First-Syllable Vowel Spellings	Examples	Second-Syllable Vowel Spellings
/ā/	*ay*	play mate	*a*-consonant-*e*
	ai	tail gate	*a*-consonant-*e*
/ē/	*ea*	sea weed	*ee*

Vowel-Sounds	First-Syllable Vowel Spellings	Examples	Second-Syllable Vowel Spellings
/ī/	*y*	sky light	*igh*
	y-consonant-*e*	type write	*i*-consonant-*e*
	i(nd)	hind sight	*igh*
	(*e* spells /e/)	neck tie	*ie*
/ō/	*ow*	tow boat	*oa*
	oe	toe hold	*o(ld)*
	ow	slow poke	*o*-consonant-*e*
/ū/ or /ü/	*ue*	blue jay	(*ay* spells /ā/)
	ui	suit case	(*a*-consonant-*e* spells /ā/)
	ew	news reel	(*ee* spells /ē/)
	u-consonant-*e*	yule tide	(*i*-consonant-*e* spells /ī/)

The long- and short-vowel spelling options will appear in various combinations in compounds. Which vowel sounds do these options spell?

First-Syllable Vowel Spellings	Examples	Second-Syllable Vowel Spellings
ai spells 1	drain pipe	*i*-consonant-*e* spells 2
ay spells 3	day dream	*ea* spells 4
ui spells 5	fruit cake	*a*-consonant-*e* spells 6
igh spells 7	sight see	*ee* spells 8
i(nd) spells 9	blind fold	*o(ld)* spells 10
ow spells 11	row boat	*oa* spells 12

First-Syllable Vowel Spellings	Examples	Second-Syllable Vowel Spellings
ay spells 13 ___	hay stack	*a* spells 14 ___
ai spells 15 ___	mail box	*o* spells 16 ___
ai spells 17 ___	paint brush	*u* spells 18 ___
ee spells 19 ___	week end	*e* spells 20 ___
u-consonant-*e* spells 21 ___	juke box	*o* spells 22 ___
ue spells 23 ___	blue print	*i* spells 24 ___
ew spells 25 ___	news cast	*a* spells 26 ___

Skill Drill 1 Write the compound words listed in the chart. Beside each word write the spelling option and sound symbol for the vowel sound in each eye-syllable. For example, write "drainpipe: 1 *ai* /ā/, 2 *i*-consonant-*e* /ī/." Check your answers at the end of Chapter 4. Be sure to write a sound symbol for each numbered line.

Skill Drill 2 Read these sound-spellings of compounds. Notice the primary and secondary accent marks. Write the regular spellings for the sound-spellings.

All the words are in the Spelling Dictionary at the back of the book. Look up any of those words you do not know.

Check your answers.

1 /sand′ bag′/
2 /shot′ gun′/
3 /jük′ boks′/
4 /līk′ wīz′/
5 /mēn′ hwīl′/
6 /blīnd′ fōld′/
7 /mī′ self′/
8 /sōp′ sudz′/
9 /kup′ kāk′/
10 /bak′ āk′/
11 /sun′ rīz′/
12 /tip′ tō′/
13 /kwik′ sand′/
14 /eg′ plant′/
15 /wich′ kraft′/
16 /skī′ līt′/
17 /fīr′ flī′/
18 /bōld′ fās′/
19 /tāl′ spin′/
20 /līv′ stok′/
21 /bēz′ waks′/
22 /blü′ gras′/
23 /with′ hōld′/
24 /flash′ līt′/
25 /tō′ bōt′/
26 /māl′ boks′/
27 /nek′ tī′/

Two-Letter Vowel Spellings in Compounds

The two-letter vowel spellings, or *digraphs— oo, ou-ow, oy-oi, au, aw,* and *a(l)*—also reappear in compounds, sometimes with the long- and short-vowel spellings. What are the missing two-letter vowel spellings in the chart?

Vowel Sounds	First-Syllable Vowel Spellings	Examples	Second-Syllable Vowel Spellings
/ü/	1	fool proof	2
/u̇/	3	cook book	4
/ou/	5	round house	6
	7	down town	8
/oi/	(*o* spells /o/)	top soil	9
	10	soy bean	(*ea* spells /ē/)
/ô/	11	sauce pan	(*a* spells /a/)
	12	saw dust	(*u* spells /u/)
	13	hall way	(*ay* spells /ā/)

Skill Drill 3 Write the compound words listed in the chart. After each one write the vowel sound symbol and the spelling option for the vowel sound. Write the spelling option for each numbered line in the chart. Check your answers.

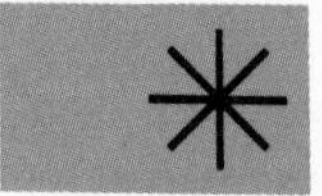

Skill Drill 4 Write the regular spellings for these sound-spellings for compound words. All the words are in the Spelling Dictionary. Look up the meaning of any word you do not know. Check your answers.

1 /nōt′ bu̇k′/	**4** /tüth′ āk′/	**7** /jig′ sô′/
2 /mün′ līt′/	**5** /hous′ wīf′/	**8** /sôft′ bôl′/
3 /out′ lô′/	**6** /oil′ klôth′/	**9** /hous′ hōld′/

10 /fīr′ prüf′/	**14** /lô′ süt′/	**18** /kount′ doun′/
11 /nīt′ goun′/	**15** /kôz′ wā′/	**19** /bel′ boi′/
12 /blō′ out′/	**16** /doun′ fôl′/	
13 /pin′ point′/	**17** /plī′ wůd′/	

Vowel-*r* Spellings in Compounds

The vowel-*r* spellings (*ar, or-ore-oar, are-air, ear-eer, er-ir-ur*) reappear in compounds also. One part of the compound may have a short- or a long-vowel spelling or a digraphic vowel spelling. What are the missing vowel-*r* spellings in the chart?

Vowel-*r* Sounds	First-Syllable Vowel-*r* Spellings	Examples	Second-Syllable Vowel-*r* Spellings
/är/	1	barn yard	2
/ôr/	3	short hand	(*a* spells /a/)
	4	fore cast	(*a* spells /a/)
	(*ar* spells /är/)	card board	5
/ãr/	6	ware house	(*ou* spells /ou/)
	7	air port	(*or* spells /ôr/)
/ir/	(*i* spells /i/)	kil deer	8
	9	ear drum	(*u* spells /u/)
/ėr/	(*i*-consonant-*e* spells /ī/)	ice berg	10
	11	birth day	(*ay* spells /ā/)
	12	turn pike	(*i*-consonant-*e* spells /ī/)

Skill Drill 5 Write the compound words in the chart. After each word write the sound symbol for the vowel-*r* sound. Then write the spelling for each numbered line for that word. Check your answers at the end of Chapter 4.

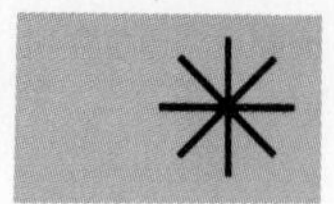

Skill Drill 6 Write the regular spellings for these compound sound-spellings. Check your answers.

1 /kär′ fãr′/
2 /pop′ kôrn′/
3 /ärm′ chãr′/
4 /stôr′ rüm′/
5 /ãr′ kraft′/
6 /hėr′ self′/
7 /sun′ bėrn′/
8 /shôrt′ stop′/
9 /fôr′ tel′/
10 /bil′ bôrd′/
11 /nīt′ mãr′/
12 /fãr′ wel′/
13 /up′ stãrz′/
14 /blü′ bėrd′/
15 /up′ rôr′/

Compounds with Snurk Spellings

In the skill drill that follows, one eye-syllable in each compound is a familiar snurk. The other eye-syllable has a regular short-vowel, long-vowel, digraphic-vowel, or vowel-*r* spelling.

Skill Drill 7 Write the compound words for these sound-spellings. All the words are in the Spelling Dictionary. Look up the meaning of any word you do not know. Check your answers.

1 /ėrth′ kwāk′/
2 /brôd′ kast′/
3 /pā′ rōl′/
4 /thrü′ out′/
5 /tuch′ doun′/
6 /chīld′ hůd′/
7 /out′ wā′/
8 /ruf′ nek′/
9 /wėrth′ hwīl′/
10 /hwīt′ wosh′/
11 /net′ wėrk′/
12 /pēs′ mēl′/
13 /vū′ point′/
14 /kôrt′ yärd′/
15 /ded′ lok′/

Summary

This chapter has reviewed compounds, or words made up of two or more smaller words. Compounds are easier to spell if they are separated into word parts. In most two-syllable compounds, each small word is an ear-syllable with a primary (louder) or secondary (softer) accent and a vowel sound that you can hear clearly. Study each word part by noting whether it has an expected or unexpected spelling. Use the same spelling options for each word part that you use for one-syllable words.

Mastery Test 4

A

For each picture, write the compound word. The vowel or vowel-*r* sounds are shown for each little word within each compound.

B

Write the missing snurk words for the sentences.

1 /sum′ tīm′/ __ /tü′ dā′/ __ I /wu̇d/ __ like a /dō′ nut′/ __.

2 /giv/ __ the /pas′ wėrd′/ __ and go /in′ tü′/ __ the /gärd′ hous′/ __.

3 I'm /lōn′ sum′/ __ and need /yu̇r/ __ /sted′ fast′/ __ /frend′ ship′/ __.

4 Read the /pōst′ skript′/ __ on this /pōst′ kärd′/ __ to /yu̇r′ self′/ __ at /wuns/ __.

5 His /yung/ __ /grand′ sun′/ __ has a /hed′ āk′/ __ and must stay /in′ dôrz′/ __.

6 Reading this /gīd′ bu̇k′/ __ will be /tīr′ sum′/ __ even for a /grāt/ __ /bu̇k′ wėrm′/ __.

7 We /hėrd/ __ news of the /ėrth′ kwāk′/ __ on a /net′ wėrk′/ __ /brôd′ kast′/ __.

8 My /frendz/ __ /thred′ bãr′/ __ /brôd′ klôth′/ __ coat is /nō′ hwãr′/ __ to be seen.

9 /hü/ __ /hwīt′ wosht′/ __ the /frunt/ __ /dôr′ step′/ __ of the /wėrk′ hous′/ __?

10 That /blud′ hound′/ __ has /bin/ __ a good /woch′ dôg′/ __ /thrü′ out′/ __ the summer.

11 It's /wėrth′ hwīl′/ __ to try for /wun/ __ more /tuch′ doun′/ __ to /sāf′ gärd′/ __ our slim lead in the game.

12 The /pach′ wėrk′/ __ quilt I /bôt/ __ is /sum′ hwot′/ __ of a /shō′ pēs′/ __.

Additional Skill Drills

Do these skill drills if you want to improve your Mastery Test score.

Additional Skill Drill 1 Print the compound words for these pictures. Mark the eye-syllables when you write the regular spellings. Check your answers at the end of the chapter.

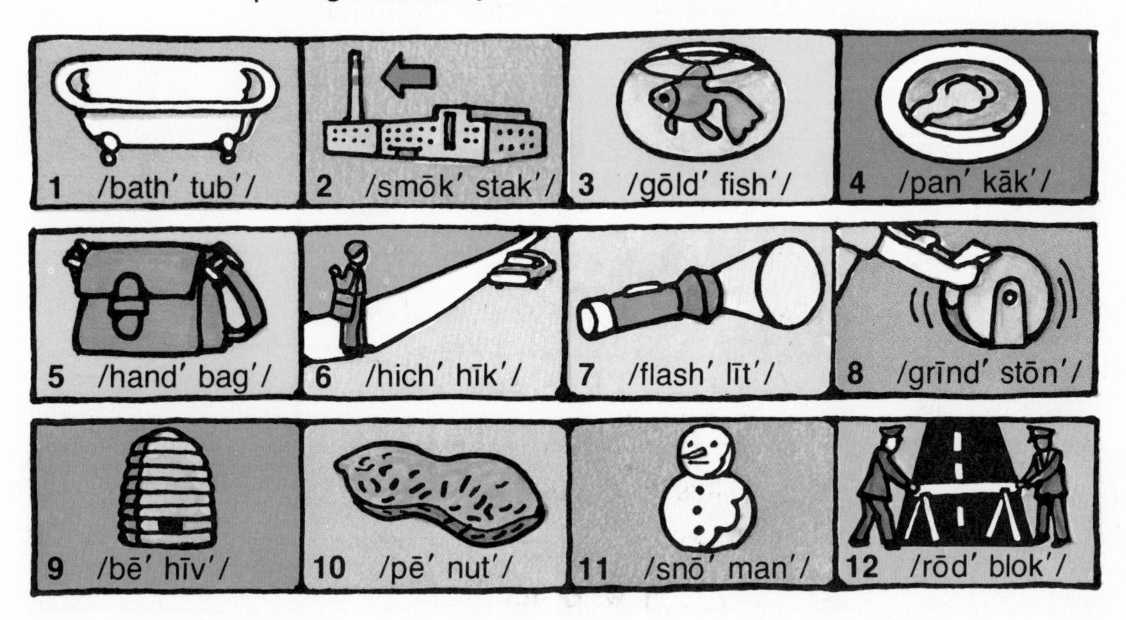

Additional Skill Drill 2 Write the compound words for these pictures. Check your answers.

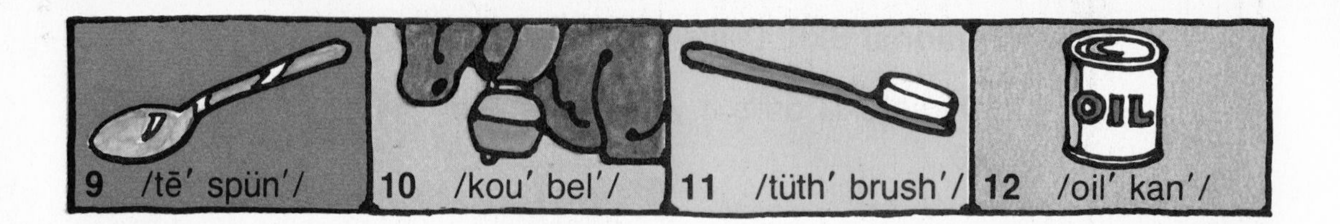

Additional Skill Drill 3 Write the vowel-*r* compounds for these pictures. Notice the primary and secondary accent marks on the ear-syllables. Check your answers.

Additional Skill Drill 4 Write the compound snurk words for these pictures. Notice the primary and secondary accent marks on the ear-syllables. Check your answers.

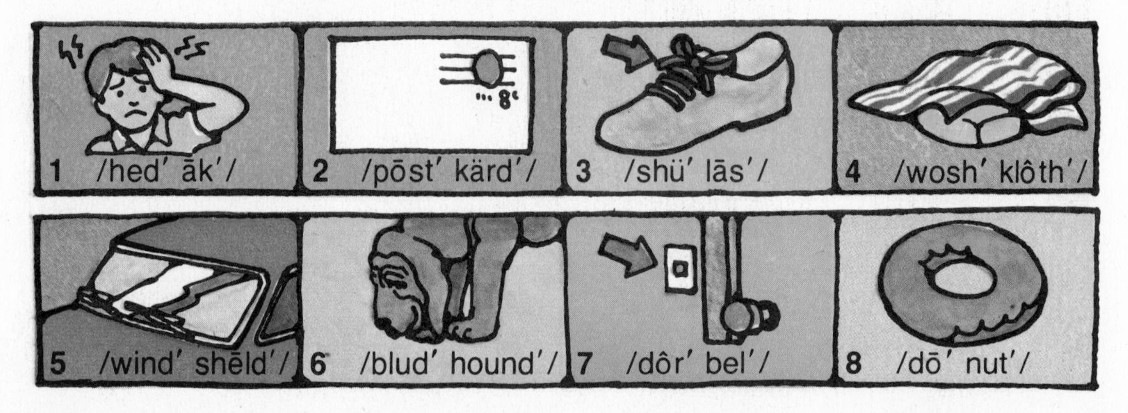

Answers for Chapter 4 Skill Drills

Skill Drill 1 Answers

drainpipe: 1 *ai* /ā/, 2 *i*-consonant-*e* /ī/
daydream: 3 *ay* /ā/, 4 *ea* /ē/
fruitcake: 5 *ui* /ü/, 6 *a*-consonant-*e* /ā/
sightsee: 7 *igh* /ī/, 8 *ee* /ē/
blindfold: 9 *i(nd)* /ī/, 10 *o(ld)* /ō/
rowboat: 11 *ow* /ō/, 12 *oa* /ō/
haystack: 13 *ay* /ā/, 14 *a* /a/
mailbox: 15 *ai* /ā/, 16 *o* /o/
paintbrush: 17 *ai* /ā/, 18 *u* /u/
weekend: 19 *ee* /ē/, 20 *e* /e/
jukebox: 21 *u*-consonant-*e* /ū/ or /ü/, 22 *o* /o/
blueprint: 23 *ue* /ü/, 24 *i* /i/
newscast: 25 *ew* /ü/, 26 *a* /a/

Skill Drill 2 Answers

1 sandbag 2 shotgun 3 jukebox 4 likewise
5 meanwhile 6 blindfold 7 myself 8 soapsuds 9 cupcake
10 backache 11 sunrise 12 tiptoe 13 quicksand
14 eggplant 15 witchcraft 16 skylight 17 firefly
18 boldface 19 tailspin 20 livestock 21 beeswax
22 bluegrass 23 withhold 24 flashlight 25 towboat
26 mailbox 27 necktie

Skill Drill 3 Answers

foolproof /ü/: 1 *oo,* 2 *oo*
cookbook /u̇/: 3 *oo,* 4 *oo*
roundhouse /ou/: 5 *ou,* 6 *ou*
downtown /ou/: 7 *ow,* 8 *ow*
topsoil /oi/: 9 *oi*
soybean /oi/: 10 *oy*
saucepan /ô/: 11 *au*
sawdust /ô/: 12 *aw*
hallway /ô/: 13 *a(l)*

Skill Drill 4 Answers

1 notebook 2 moonlight 3 outlaw 4 toothache
5 housewife 6 oilcloth 7 jigsaw 8 softball
9 household 10 fireproof 11 nightgown 12 blowout
13 pinpoint 14 lawsuit 15 causeway 16 downfall
17 plywood 18 countdown 19 bellboy

Skill Drill 5 Answers

barnyard /är/: 1 *ar,* 2 *ar*
shorthand /ôr/: 3 *or*
forecast /ôr/: 4 *ore*
cardboard /ôr/: 5 *oar*
warehouse /ãr/: 6 *are*
airport /ãr/: 7 *air*
kildeer /ir/: 8 *eer*
eardrum /ir/: 9 *ear*
iceberg /ėr/: 10 *er*
birthday /ėr/: 11 *ir*
turnpike /ėr/: 12 *ur*

Skill Drill 6 Answers

1 carfare 2 popcorn 3 armchair 4 storeroom
5 aircraft 6 herself 7 sunburn 8 shortstop 9 foretell
10 billboard 11 nightmare 12 farewell 13 upstairs
14 bluebird 15 uproar

Skill Drill 7 Answers

1 earthquake 2 broadcast 3 payroll 4 throughout
5 touchdown 6 childhood 7 outweigh 8 roughneck
9 worthwhile 10 whitewash 11 network 12 piecemeal
13 viewpoint 14 courtyard 15 deadlock

Answers for Chapter 4 Additional Skill Drills

Additional Skill Drill 1 Answers

1 bath tub 2 smoke stack 3 gold fish 4 pan cake

5 hand bag 6 hitch hike 7 flash light 8 grind stone
9 bee hive 10 pea nut 11 snow man 12 road block

Additional Skill Drill 2 Answers

1 footstool 2 bookcase 3 baseball 4 toadstool
5 footprint 6 whiskbroom 7 suitcase 8 snowplow
9 teaspoon 10 cowbell 11 toothbrush 12 oilcan

Additional Skill Drill 3 Answers

1 cartwheel 2 scoreboard 3 corkscrew 4 scarecrow
5 hairpin 6 sideburns 7 wheelchair 8 trademark
9 surfboard 10 pitchfork 11 turnstile 12 switchboard

Additional Skill Drill 4 Answers

1 headache 2 postcard 3 shoelace 4 washcloth
5 windshield 6 bloodhound 7 doorbell 8 doughnut

5 Spelling Soft Syllable Endings

The dictionaries show the syllables of longer words in three degrees of loudness. A primary stress mark, or accent mark, shows the loudest syllable, a secondary stress mark shows that a syllable is less loud, and no stress mark at all shows that a syllable is spoken still more softly. When you say syllables with no stress, you can still hear the consonant sounds clearly, but the vowel sounds become very soft. Many words are hard to spell because you cannot hear the vowel sounds in the soft, or unstressed, syllables. This chapter reviews three common word endings that have no stress. Each of the three endings has several spelling options.

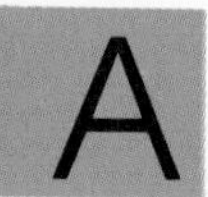

The /ē/ Spelling Options

Almost all the compound words in Chapter 4 have one ear-syllable with primary stress and one ear-syllable with secondary stress. Many two-syllable words have one loud syllable with primary stress and one syllable spoken so softly that the dictionary shows no stress mark, or accent mark, with it. The two-syllable words in which *y* or *ey* spells the unstressed /ē/ ending are examples of such words.

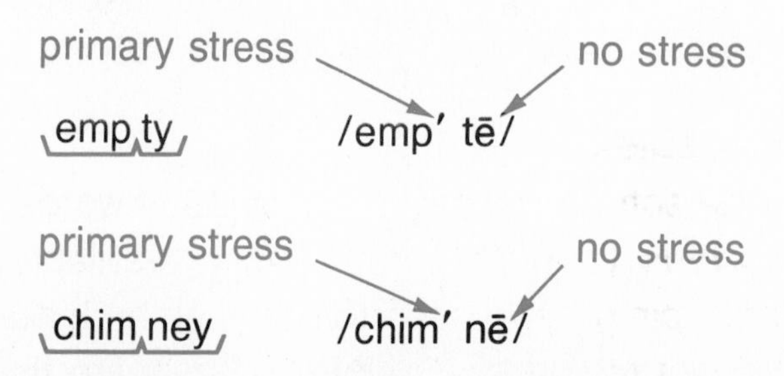

The *y* and *ey* spellings are the two main spelling options for these /ē/-ending words. (A few words like *brownie, prairie, collie, dogie, genie,* and *movie* have the *ie* spelling for the soft /ē/ ending, and *caddie* and *cookie* are also spelled *caddy* [tea box] and *cooky.*)

1 The *ey* Spellings

There are hundreds of *y*-ending words and relatively few *ey* spellings. Become familiar with these few *ey* words. Some have snurk spellings in the loud, or stressed, syllables.

Sometimes a consonant sound goes with the /ē/ syllable and sometimes it does not. When there is more than one consonant sound in the middle of a word, the ear-syllables are usually divided between the consonant sounds.

Be sure you know the meanings of these words. Look up the meanings of unfamiliar words in the Spelling Dictionary at the back of the book.

don key	/dong′ kē/	kid ney	/kid′ nē/
mon key	/mung′ kē/	med ley	/med′ lē/
hock ey	/hok′ ē/	tur key	/tėr′ kē/
jock ey	/jok′ ē/	par ley	/pär′ lē/
jer sey	/jėr′ zē/	par sley	/pär′ slē/

Skill Drill 1 Write the *ey*-ending words for these sound-spellings. Check your answers at the end of the chapter.

1 /vol′ ē/	**4** /al′ ē/	**7** /hun′ ē/
2 /bär′ lē/	**5** /val′ ē/	**8** /mun′ ē/
3 /chim′ nē/	**6** /gal′ ē/	**9** /jėr′ nē/

2 Eye-Syllables for *y*-Ending Words

We spell the soft /ē/ ending of hundreds of words with *y. Look* at these words to see the parts, or eye-syllables. The eye-syllables are simply the best grouping of the letters of a word in order to *see* the parts. The ear-syllables are the word parts you *hear* when you *say* the word. Sometimes the eye-syllables and ear-syllables agree, but sometimes they do not.

In some *y*-ending words, the consonant letter (or letters) before the *y* goes with the last eye-syllable. When there are doubled consonant letters before *y,* we usually divide the eye-syllables between the two consonant letters as a reminder that there are doubled consonant letters in the spelling. Notice the eye-syllables in the words below.

jel ly quar ry diz zy

But you *say* only one of the consonant sounds when you speak the words, as the dictionary shows in the ear-syllables.

jel ly /jel′ ē/ quar ry /kwär′ ē/ diz zy /diz′ ē/

When two different consonant letters come before the *y,* we generally divide the eye-syllables between the two consonant letters and divide the ear-syllables between the two consonant sounds.

fif ty /fif′ tē/ en vy /en′ vē/ mer cy /mėr′ sē/

But when two consonant letters spell one sound, we do not separate them in the eye-syllables.

flash y /flash′ ē/ stick y /stik′ ē/ tro phy /trō′ fē/

When the first syllable is a familiar word, it is often best to keep it as a whole eye-syllable. The familiar word may be divided, however, in the ear-syllables.

fault y /fôl′ tē/ part y /pär′ tē/ might y /mī′ tē/

Skill Drill 2 Write the regular spellings for these consonant-*y*–ending words. Check your answers with those at the end of Chapter 5.

1 /fôr′ tē/	**4** /stud′ ē/	**7** /sil′ ē/
2 /twen′ tē/	**5** /lā′ dē/	**8** /jol′ ē/
3 /fun′ ē/	**6** /krā′ zē/	**9** /noi′ zē/

3 Plural Forms of *y*- and *ey*-Ending Nouns

The spelling of plural noun forms of *ey*-ending words is easy because you simply add *s* to form the plurals.

chimney chimney*s*

To spell the plural forms of words ending in consonant-letter–*y*, change *y* to *i* and add *es*.

berry berr*ies* county count*ies* copy cop*ies*

Skill Drill 3 Write the spellings for the plural noun forms of these /ē/-ending words. Look up any word you do not know.

1 /dü' tē/	**4** /gul' ē/	**7** /en' trē/
2 /med' lē/	**5** /kid' nē/	**8** /jėr' nē/
3 /pär' tē/	**6** /fol' ē/	**9** /jür' ē/

4 Adding *es* and *ed* to *y*-Ending Verbs

Change the final *y* to *i* before adding the *es* and *ed* verb endings.

▽ bury	envy	▽ rally
▽ bur*ies*	env*ies*	▽ rall*ies*
▽ bur*ied*	env*ied*	▽ rall*ied*

Skill Drill 4 Write the spellings for the *es* and *ed* verb forms of these words. The words are in the Spelling Dictionary.

1 /kėr' ē/	**4** /hėr' ē/	**7** /ral' ē/
2 /pit' ē/	**5** /wėr' ē/	**8** /en' vē/
3 /fan' sē/	**6** /kop' ē/	**9** /skėr' ē/

5 Adding *er* and *est* to *y*-Ending Adjectives

Also change the final *y* to *i* before adding the *er* and *est* endings to *y*-ending adjectives.

chilly	dirty	lucky
chill*ier*	dirt*ier*	luck*ier*
chill*iest*	dirt*iest*	luck*iest*

Skill Drill 5 Write the regular spellings of these words and their *er* and *est* adjective forms. Check your answers.

1 /bul′ kē/ **3** /grē′ dē/ **5** /noi′ zē/
2 /biz′ ē/ **4** /ē′ zē/ **6** /wir′ ē/

6 The *y*-Ending Snurks

The great majority of final-*y* words have regular, or expected, spellings of the stressed first syllable. Here is a list of common *y*-ending words that have snurk spellings of the stressed ear-syllables. The words are in the Spelling Dictionary.

- healthy /hel′ thē/
- heavy /hev′ ē/
- ready /red′ ē/
- early /ėr′ lē/
- busy /biz′ ē/
- country /kun′ trē/
- fully /fu̇l′ ē/
- bushy /bu̇sh′ ē/
- only /ōn′ lē/
- guilty /gil′ tē/
- eighty /ā′ tē/
- wealthy /wel′ thē/
- hearty /här′ tē/
- poultry /pōl′ trē/
- query /kwir′ ē/
- tally /tal′ ē/
- rally /ral′ ē/
- bully /bu̇l′ ē/

The /əl/ Spelling Options

Another soft, or unstressed, ending is the /əl/ ending. Some dictionaries show the ending as /l/. Others show it as /əl/. The /ə/ symbol, the *schwa* (/shwä/), is used by dictionaries to show the soft vowel sound in many unstressed syllables. These unstressed syllables are said so softly and quickly that the vowel sound almost disappears. This soft vowel sound may be spelled with any of the five vowel letters.

a spells /ə/	a bout	/ə bout′/
e spells /ə/	ta ken	/tā′ kən/
i spells /ə/	pen cil	/pen′ səl/
o spells /ə/	lem on	/lem′ ən/
u spells /ə/	cir cus	/sėr′ kəs/

There are seven spelling options for the /əl/ ending. Sometimes the preceding consonant sound goes with the /əl/ in ear-syllables, but often it does not.

le	*el*	*al*	*ol*
ta ble	lev el	ri val	i dol
/tā' bəl/	/lev' əl/	/rī' vəl/	/ī' dəl/

il	*ile*	*ul*
e vil	rep tile	con sul
/ē' vəl/	/rep' təl/	/kon' səl/

The majority of the /əl/-ending words are spelled with *le,* but there are many *el* and *al* spellings also. There are several *il* and *ile* spellings and a few *ol* spellings. There are not enough *ul* spellings to cause trouble.

1 The *el* Spelling Option

To avoid spelling errors in words with the /əl/ ending, become familiar with the most commonly used *el* words. Notice that the vowel sounds in the stressed first syllables of these forty-two *el* words repeat the familiar spelling patterns of one-syllable words. If you do not know the meaning of any of the words, look it up in the Spelling Dictionary.

/a/	/e/	/i/	/o/
cam el	ken nel	chis el	gos pel
can cel	lev el	shriv el	mon grel
chan nel	rev el	tin sel	mod el
chap el	reb el		pom mel
dam sel	ves sel		
flan nel			
gav el			
rav el	/u/	/ā/	/ē/
trav el	cud gel	ha zel	ea sel
pan el	tun nel	la bel	se quel
tas sel	pum mel		

/ō/	/ū/	/ü/	/ou/
yo del	fu el	jew el	tow el
		cru el	vow el
			scoun drel

/är/	/ôr/	/ėr/
mar vel	mor sel	squir rel
par cel	snor kel	

Skill Drill 6 Write the spellings for these *el*-ending words.

1 /fun′ əl/	**4** /kwär′ əl/	**7** /nik′ əl/
2 /pret′ zəl/	**5** /grav′ əl/	**8** /dü′ əl/
3 /wē′ zəl/	**6** /nov′ əl/	**9** /trou′ əl/

2 The *al* Spelling Option

Study the eye-syllables of these forty-one common words with the *al* spelling of /əl/. The words are in the Spelling Dictionary.

/a/	/e/	/i/	/ā/
scan dal	pet al	dis mal	fa tal
van dal	men tal	crys tal	na sal
ras cal	rent al	hym nal	**/ē/**
vas sal	cen tral		le gal
jack al			e qual

/ī/	/ō/	/ū/	/ôr/
fi nal	lo cal	mu ral	flor al
spi nal	vo cal		mor al
ti dal	coast al		or al
tri bal	o pal		nor mal
spi ral	o val		mor tal
vi tal			por tal
di al			

/oi/	/ü/	/är/	/ėr/
loy al	bru tal	mar shal	ver bal
roy al	fru gal		

Skill Drill 7 Write the spellings for these *al*-ending words. Check your answers.

1 /rī′ vəl/
2 /trī′ əl/
3 /fôr′ məl/
4 /mam′ əl/
5 /rủr′ əl/
6 /den′ təl/
7 /san′ dəl/
8 /tō′ təl/
9 /sig′ nəl/

3 The *il* and *ile* Spelling Options

There are relatively few words with the *il* and *ile* spellings of /əl/. Learn these words.

il Endings	*ile* Endings
an vil	ag ile
dev il	frag ile
e vil	fu tile
fos sil	mo bile
per il	ster ile
len til	text ile
sten cil	
ten dril	
ton sil	
nos tril	
vig il	
tran quil	
wee vil	

Skill Drill 8 Write the regular spellings for these *il*- and *ile*-ending words. Check your answers.

1 /pū′ pəl/
2 /pen′ səl/
3 /rep′ təl/
4 /siv′ əl/
5 /fėr′ təl/
6 /fū′ təl/

4 The /əl/ Homonyms

There are a number of /əl/ homonyms that may cause spelling difficulties. All the common *ol* spellings, for example, have homonyms.

Learn the following homonym pairs.

cymbal (brass plate)
symbol (sign)

duel (fight)
dual (double)

medal (stamped metal)
meddle (interfere)

metal (iron, etc.)
mettle (courage)

pedal (foot lever)
peddle (sell)

counsel (advise)
council (advisory group)

hostel (inn)
hostile (unfriendly)

kernel (center part)
colonel (officer)

mantel (fireplace shelf)
mantle (cloak)

pistol (gun)
pistil (flower part)

gambol (play)
gamble (risk)

idol (image)
idle (not busy)

missile (rocket)
missal (prayer book)

Skill Drill 9 Write the missing /əl/ homonym for each sentence.

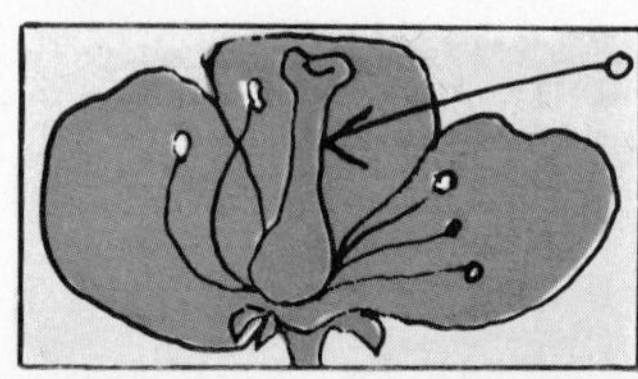

1 This part is the ___.

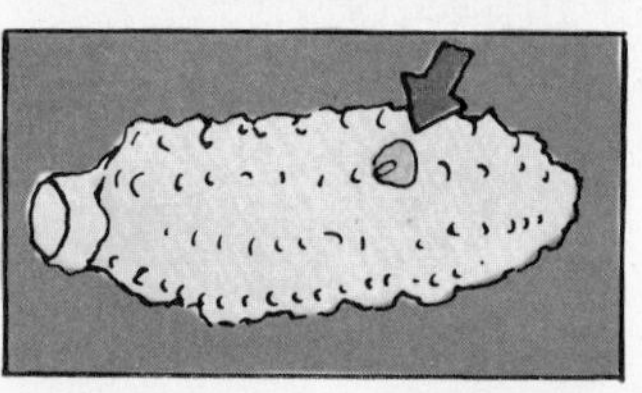

2 That's the ___.

3 They certainly are ___.

4 The __ is meeting.

5 He's wearing a __.

6 She's banging the __.

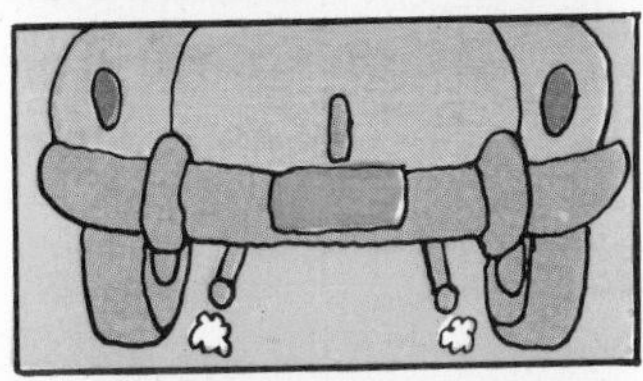

7 There are __ pipes.

8 That's an __.

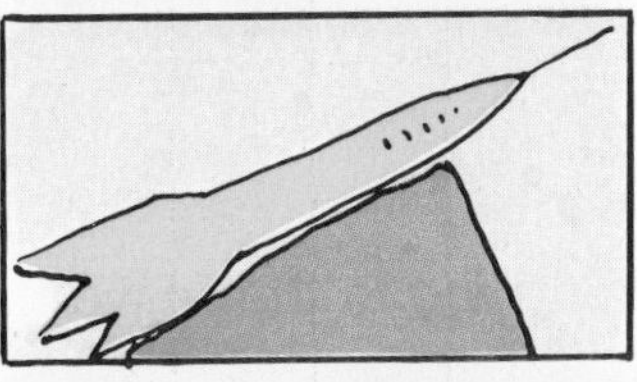

9 And this is a __.

10 He's missing a __.

11 She's being awarded a __.

12 There's a lot of old __ there.

5 The /əl/ Snurks

There are unexpected spellings, or snurks, in some of the /əl/-ending words. Look up any meanings you do not know.

le Snurks	*el* Snurks	*al* Snurks
coup le	an gel	plur al
doub le	bush el	rur al
troub le	bar rel	post al
wad dle	die sel	
squab ble	grov el	
tread le	hov el	
mus cle	shov el	

Skill Drill 10 Write the /əl/ snurks for these sound-spellings. Check your answers.

1 /trub′ əl/	**4** /bar′ əl/	**7** /kup′ əl/
2 /ān′ jəl/	**5** /bu̇sh′ əl/	**8** /shuv′ əl/
3 /plu̇r′ əl/	**6** /dub′ əl/	**9** /pōst′ əl/

6 Adding *ing* to /əl/ Words

Drop the final *e* before adding *ing* to the *le* words, as with one-syllable words.

com*e*	handl*e*	wrestl*e*
coming	handling	wrestling

Remember that when one-syllable words end with a single vowel and a single consonant letter, you double the final consonant letter before adding *ing*.

bat	dig	stop
bat*ting*	dig*ging*	stop*ping*

Also, when two-syllable vowel-*l* words have stress on the *second* syllable, you double the final consonant letter before adding *ing.*

rebel /rē bel′/
rebel*ling*

control /kən trōl′/
control*ling*

But since the stress is *not* on the second syllable in an /əl/-ending vowel-*l* word, do *not* double the final consonant letter before adding *ing.*

level /lev′ əl/
level*ing*

pedal /ped′ əl/
pedal*ing*

carol /kar′ əl/
carol*ing*

equal /ē′ kwəl/
equal*ing*

Skill Drill 11 Write the *ing* forms for these /əl/-ending words. Check your answers.

1 /rī′ vəl/
2 /yō′ dəl/
3 /driz′ əl/
4 /kin′ dəl/
5 /tō′ təl/
6 /spī′ rəl/
7 /trav′ əl/
8 /kwär′ əl/
9 /stärt′ əl/

The /ər/ Spelling Options

The third soft, or unstressed, syllable ending that may cause spelling errors is the /ər/ ending. The /ər/ is softer than the /ėr/ sounds in stressed syllables, and the spelling options are different. The expected spellings of stressed vowel-*r* /ėr/ syllables are *er* (her), *ir* (sir), and *ur* (fur). The spelling options for the unstressed /ər/ syllable are generally *er, ar,* and *or.* (There are a few *ur* spellings *[murmur, sulfur],* a few *re* spellings *[acre, ogre],* and a few *yr* spellings *[zephyr, martyr]* of the /ər/ ending.) The *er* spellings of /ər/ are far more numerous than all the other /ər/ spellings combined. If you center attention upon the two-syllable words with *ar* and *or* spellings, you may be fairly sure that the other /ər/ words will be spelled *er.*

1 The *or* Spelling Option

There are about twice as many *or* spellings as *ar* spellings for /ər/. The *or* words have the usual variety of vowel spellings in the stressed syllables. All the words listed here are in the Spelling Dictionary. If you do not know the meanings, you may look them up there.

cap tor	spon sor	do nor
fac tor	con dor	ro tor
pas tor	sculp tor	o dor
trac tor	suc cor	tu tor
cam phor	tai lor	hu mor
clam or	fla vor	ru mor
ten or	fa vor	tu mor
sect or	la bor	suit or
splen dor	ma jor	stu por
trem or	sa vor	fer vor
scis sors	va por	ar bor
vic tor	vi sor	har bor
vig or	mi nor	hor ror

Snurks

err or	debt or	val or
ter ror	jur or	li quor
mir ror	hon or	

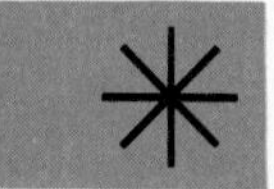

Skill Drill 12 Read these sound-spellings. Write the *or*-ending word for each of the sound-spellings. After you have written the words, check your answers with those at the end of the chapter.

1 /ak′ tər/	**7** /rā′ zər/	**13** /ang′ kər/
2 /dok′ tər/	**8** /är′ mər/	**14** /sā′ lər/
3 /mā′ ər/	**9** /mō′ tər/	**15** /ô′ thər/
4 /mī′ nər/	**10** /rü′ mər/	**16** /ter′ ər/
5 /tā′ lər/	**11** /lā′ bər/	**17** /skulp′ tər/
6 /kam′ fər/	**12** /siz′ ərz/	**18** /det′ ər/

2 The *ar* Spelling Option

Learn these words that have the *ar* spelling option.

gram mar
beg gar
nec tar
pil lar
vic ar
schol ar
dol lar
pop lar
vul gar
ce dar
fri ar
so lar
mo lar
lu nar
mor tar

Snurks

▽ sug ar
▽ cou gar

Skill Drill 13 Write the regular spellings for these *ar*-ending words.

1 /pō′ lər/
2 /sel′ ər/
3 /kol′ ər/
4 /lī′ ər/
5 /bėr′ glər/
6 /sē′ dər/

3 The *er* Snurks

There are hundreds of two-syllable words with *er* endings. Many are snurks because of unexpected spellings in their stressed syllables. Important *er* snurks are listed here.

▽ great er
▽ break er
▽ clean ser
▽ sweat er
▽ leath er
▽ weath er
▽ post er
▽ ko sher
▽ hol ster
▽ bol ster
▽ hov er
▽ won der
▽ oth er
▽ broth er
▽ smoth er
▽ boul der
▽ shoul der
▽ sol dier
▽ fath er
▽ watch er
▽ cham ber
▽ laugh ter
▽ squan der
▽ con quer
▽ an swer
▽ build er
▽ field er
▽ wie ner
▽ freight er
▽ heif er
▽ buy er
▽ gey ser

Skill Drill 14 Write the *er*-ending snurks for these sound-spellings. Check your answers.

1 /feᴛʜ′ ər/
2 /kuv′ ər/
3 /muᴛʜ′ ər/
4 /an′ sər/
5 /wosh′ ər/
6 /bī′ ər/

4 The *ng* Spellings

You have learned that to spell the /ng/ sound we use *ng* or we use *n* before a /k/ sound. The *n* spells /ng/ before /k/ in words like *banker* /bang′ kər/, *blinker* /bling′ kər/, *bunker* /bung′ kər/, *anchor* /ang′ kər/, and *rancor* /rang′ kər/.

We expect *ng* to spell /ng/ as it does in these *er* words.

sing er /sing′ ər/
ring er /ring′ ər/
young ster /yung′ stər/
string er /string′ ər/
hang er /hang′ ər/

In another group of *er* words, *ng* spells the /n/ and /j/ sounds.

gin ger /jin′ jər/
man ger /mān′ jər/
ran ger /rān′ jər/
plun ger /plun′ jər/

And in another group of *er* words, *ng* spells /ng/ and /g/.

fing er /fing′ gər/
strong er /strông′ gər/
ling er /ling′ gər/
young er /yung′ gər/

Skill Drill 15 Write the sound-spellings for these *ng* words.

1 longer
2 danger
3 stinger
4 hunger
5 stranger
6 ringer

5 The /ər/ Homonyms

There are a few homonym groups among the /ər/-ending words. Review these pairs of homonyms and notice the differences in meaning and spelling.

hanger (for clothing)
hangar (to house airplanes)

miner (one who mines)
minor (lesser, younger)

alter (change)
altar (in church)

ringer (in horseshoes)
wringer (for wet clothing)

manor (large estate)
manner (way of doing)

better (superior)
bettor (one who bets)

Skill Drill 16 Write the correct /ər/ homonyms for these picture words. Check your answers with the list or at the end of Chapter 5.

1 He has a polite ___.

2 She is a ___.

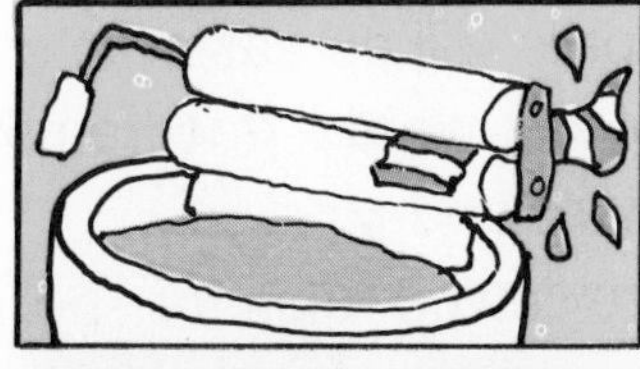

3 This is a ___.

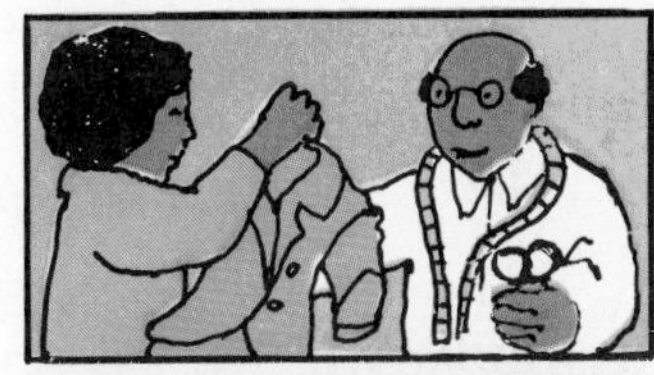

4 Please ___ it.

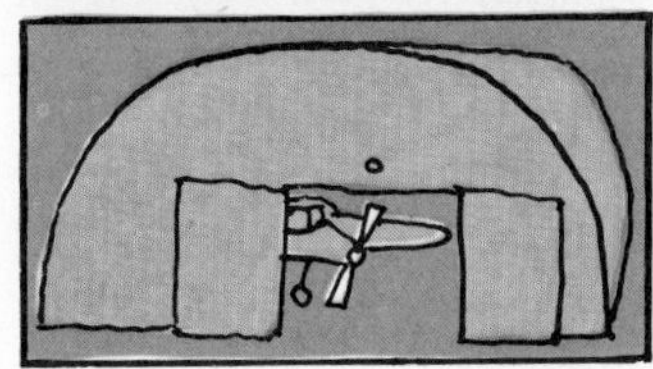

5 This is a ___.

Skill Drill 17 Write the /ər/ snurks for these sound-spellings. Check your answers.

1 /mir′ ər/
2 /shu̇g′ ər/
3 /klen′ zər/
4 /swet′ ər/
5 /kü′ gər/
6 /on′ ər/
7 /feᴛʜ′ ər/
8 /kuv′ ər/
9 /lik′ ər/
10 /bōl′ dər/
11 /wun′ dər/
12 /det′ ər/
13 /uᴛʜ′ ər/
14 /shōl′ dər/
15 /nā′ bər/
16 /sōl′ jər/
17 /laf′ tər/
18 /an′ sər/
19 /kong′ kər/
20 /bil′ dər/
21 /brā′ kər/

Summary

This chapter has reviewed two-syllable words in which the second syllable is spoken so softly that the dictionary shows it with no accent mark. Attention was given to three groups of such soft-syllable words: (1) /ē/-ending words in which the final syllable ends with *ey* or with a consonant and *y,* (2) words that end with /əl/, and (3) words that end with /ər/.

In words with /əl/ or /ər/ endings, the vowel sound in the final syllable is spoken quickly and softly. No matter how the vowel sound is spelled in an /əl/ or /ər/ syllable, it always has the blurred sound that the dictionary shows with the schwa symbol: /ə/.

The soft-/ē/-ending words will be easier to spell if you learn the relatively short list of *ey* words and remember that the others end with a consonant and *y.*

This chapter has also reviewed rules for spelling /ē/-ending words to which *s, es, ed, er,* and *est* are added: (1) To spell the plural form of consonant-*y* nouns or the *es* form of consonant-*y* verbs, change the *y* to *i* and add *es (berry, berries; bury, buries).* (2) To spell the plural forms of *ey* nouns, add *s (valley, valleys; monkey, monkeys).* (3) To spell the *er* and *est* forms of consonant-*y* adjectives and the *ed* forms of consonant-*y* verbs, change the *y* to *i* and add the ending *(pretty, prettier, prettiest; worry, worried).*

Mastery Test 5

A

Each pair of words consists of an adjective and a noun that the adjective describes. Spell each pair of words correctly.

1 /līv′ lē/ /mung′ kē/
2 /noi′ zē/ /sit′ ē/
3 /stėr′ dē/ /pō′ nē/
4 /stik′ ē/ /hun′ ē/
5 /biz′ ē/ /jėr′ nē/
6 /glü′ mē/ /val′ ē/
7 /kėr′ lē/ /pär′ slē/
8 /klum′ zē/ /dong′ kē/
9 /ē′ zē/ /dū′ tē/
10 /fôl′ tē/ /pu̇l′ ē/
11 /tī′ nē/ /cher′ ē/
12 /drou′ zē/ /bā′ bē/
13 /ru̇r′ əl/ /huv′ əl/
14 /fā′ təl/ /dü′ əl/
15 /roi′ əl/ /jü′ əlz/
16 /lit′ əl/ /ras′ kəl/
17 /dub′ əl/ /tas′ əl/
18 /fē′ bəl/ /mong′ grəl/
19 /fraj′ əl/ /tin′ səl/
20 /aj′ əl/ /skwėr′ əl/
21 /trang′ kwəl/ /chap′ əl/
22 /mod′ əl/ /pū′ pəl/
23 /mär′ bəl/ /ī′ dəl/
24 /här′ dər/ /lā′ bər/
25 /lông′ gər/ /an′ sər/
26 /pō′ lər/ /här′ bər/
27 /wärm′ ər/ /weŦH′ ər/
28 /mī′ nər/ /ak′ tər/
29 /ōl′ dər/ /trak′ tər/
30 /vul′ gər/ /beg′ ər/
31 /uŦH′ ər/ /siz′ ərz/
32 /sē′ dər/ /pil′ ər/
33 /swē′ tər/ /nek′ tər/
34 /bet′ ər/ /mā′ ər/
35 /mā′ jər/ /er′ ər/

B

Spell each word correctly with the *s* or *es* verb ending.

1 /kop′ ē/
2 /sig′ nəl/
3 /smuŦH′ ər/
4 /en′ vē/
5 /trav′ əl/
6 /wėr′ ē/

Spell each word correctly with the *est* adjective ending.

7 /stik′ ē/
8 /krü′ əl/
9 /gil′ tē/
10 /wel′ thē/
11 /brit′ əl/
12 /sim′ pəl/

Spell each word correctly with the *ing* verb ending.

13 /rē bel′/
14 /lā′ bər/
15 /yō′ dəl/
16 /gig′ əl/
17 /ē′ kwəl/
18 /kən trōl′/

Spell the plural form of each word.

Additional Skill Drills

Do these skill drills if you want to improve your Mastery Test score.

Additional Skill Drill 1 Write the spellings for these /ē/-ending words. Use the lists in the chapter if you need to. Check your answers.

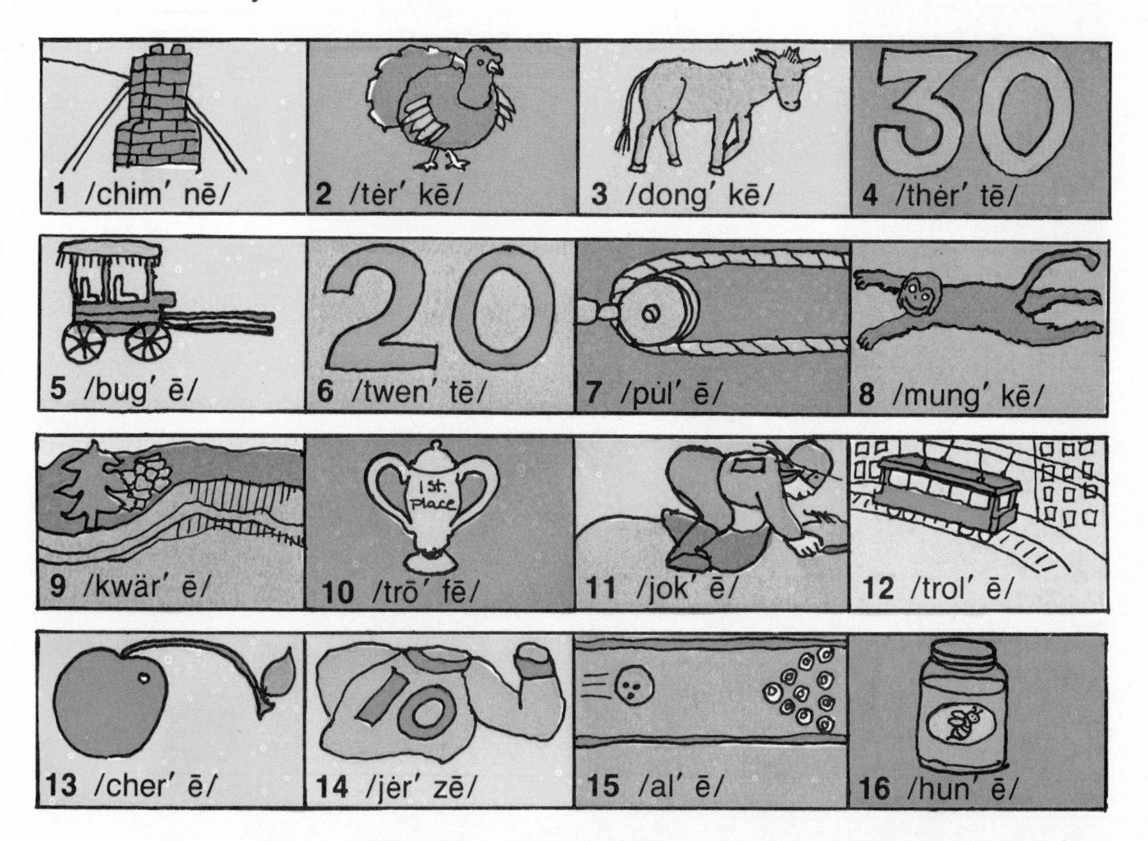

Additional Skill Drill 2 Write the regular spellings for these /əl/ words. The words have *le, al, el,* and *il* endings. Check your answers.

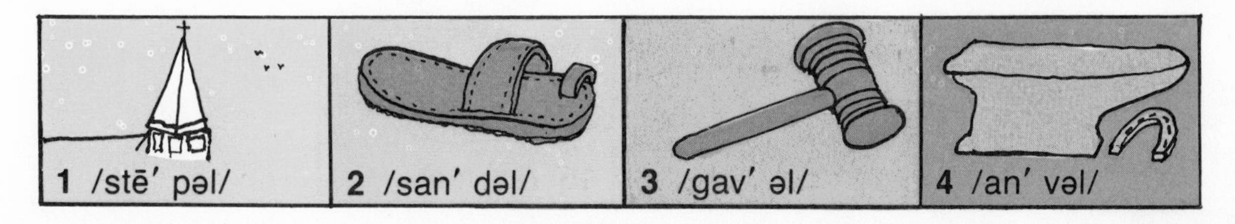

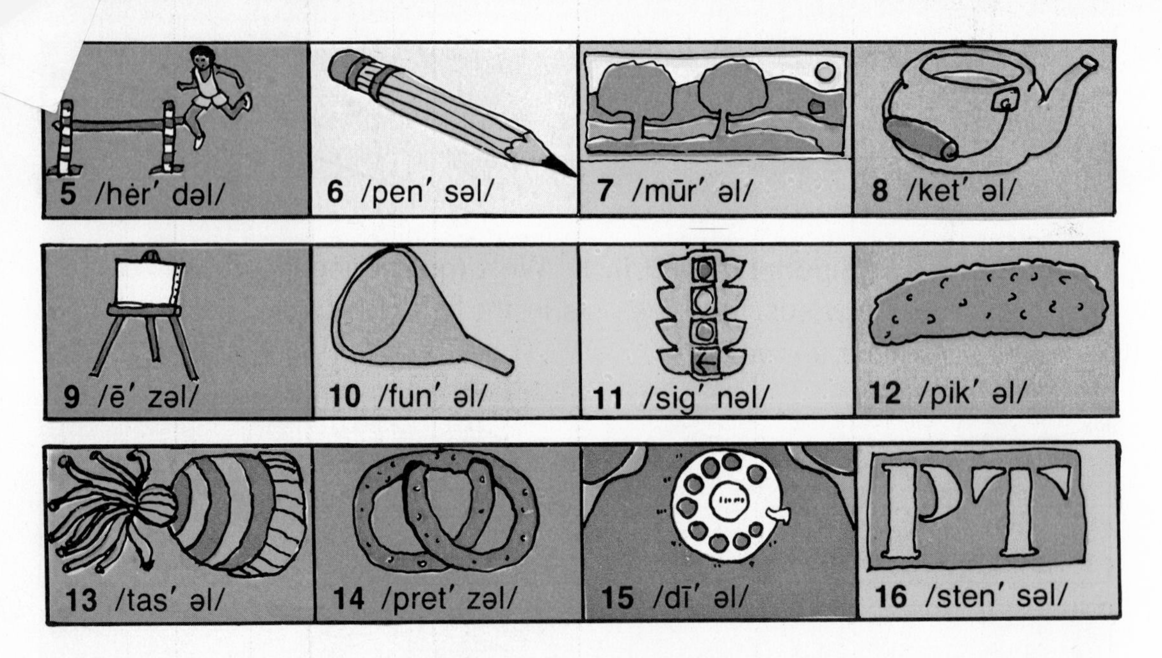

Additional Skill Drill 3 Write the /ər/-ending picture words. Check your answers.

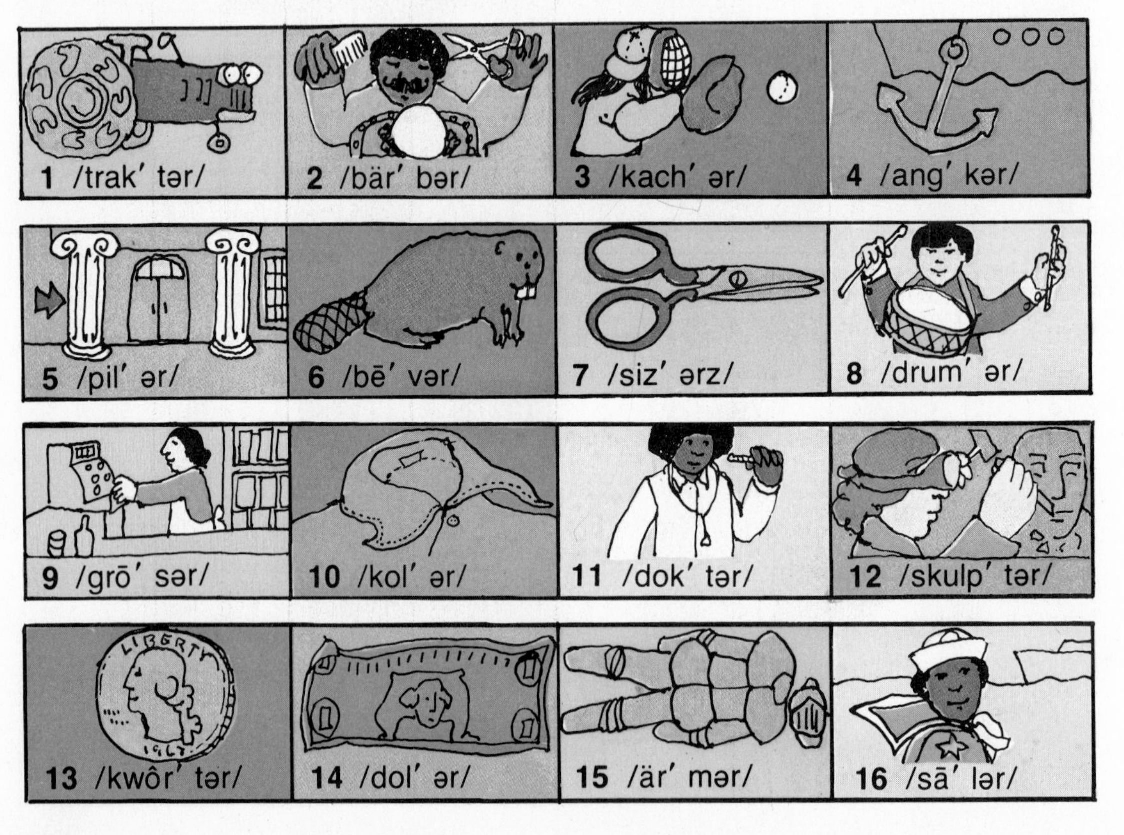

Answers for Chapter 5 Skill Drills

Skill Drill 1 Answers

1 volley 2 barley 3 chimney 4 alley 5 valley
6 galley 7 honey 8 money 9 journey

Skill Drill 2 Answers

1 forty 2 twenty 3 funny 4 study 5 lady 6 crazy
7 silly 8 jolly 9 noisy

Skill Drill 3 Answers

1 duties 2 medleys 3 parties 4 gullies 5 kidneys
6 follies 7 entries 8 journeys 9 juries

Skill Drill 4 Answers

1 curries, curried 2 pities, pitied 3 fancies, fancied
4 hurries, hurried 5 worries, worried 6 copies, copied
7 rallies, rallied 8 envies, envied 9 scurries, scurried

Skill Drill 5 Answers

1 bulky, bulkier, bulkiest 2 busy, busier, busiest
3 greedy, greedier, greediest 4 easy, easier, easiest
5 noisy, noisier, noisiest 6 weary, wearier, weariest

Skill Drill 6 Answers

1 funnel 2 pretzel 3 weasel 4 quarrel 5 gravel
6 novel 7 nickel 8 duel 9 trowel

Skill Drill 7 Answers

1 rival 2 trial 3 formal 4 mammal 5 rural 6 dental
7 sandal 8 total 9 signal

Skill Drill 8 Answers

1 pupil 2 pencil 3 reptile 4 civil 5 fertile 6 futile

Skill Drill 9 Answers

1 pistil 2 kernel 3 hostile 4 council 5 mantle
6 cymbal 7 dual 8 idol 9 missile 10 pedal
11 medal 12 metal

Skill Drill 10 Answers

1 trouble 2 angel 3 plural 4 barrel 5 bushel
6 double 7 couple 8 shovel 9 postal

Skill Drill 11 Answers

1 rivaling 2 yodeling 3 drizzling 4 kindling 5 totaling
6 spiraling 7 traveling 8 quarreling 9 startling

Skill Drill 12 Answers

1 actor 2 doctor 3 mayor 4 minor 5 tailor
6 camphor 7 razor 8 armor 9 motor 10 rumor
11 labor 12 scissors 13 anchor 14 sailor 15 author
16 terror 17 sculptor 18 debtor

Skill Drill 13 Answers

1 polar 2 cellar 3 collar 4 liar 5 burglar 6 cedar

Skill Drill 14 Answers

1 feather 2 cover 3 mother 4 answer 5 washer
6 buyer

Skill Drill 15 Answers

1 /lông′ gər/ 2 /dān′ jər/ 3 /sting′ ər/ 4 /hung′ gər/
5 /strān′ jər/ 6 /ring′ ər/

Skill Drill 16 Answers

1 manner 2 miner 3 wringer 4 alter 5 hangar

Skill Drill 17 Answers

1 mirror 2 sugar 3 cleanser 4 sweater 5 cougar
6 honor 7 feather 8 cover 9 liquor 10 boulder
11 wonder 12 debtor 13 other 14 shoulder 15 neighbor
16 soldier 17 laughter 18 answer 19 conquer 20 builder
21 breaker

Answers for Chapter 5 Additional Skill Drills

Additional Skill Drill 1 Answers

1 chimney 2 turkey 3 donkey 4 thirty 5 buggy
6 twenty 7 pulley 8 monkey 9 quarry 10 trophy

11 jockey 12 trolley 13 cherry 14 jersey 15 alley
16 honey

Additional Skill Drill 2 Answers

1 steeple 2 sandal 3 gavel 4 anvil 5 hurdle
6 pencil 7 mural 8 kettle 9 easel 10 funnel 11 signal
12 pickle 13 tassel 14 pretzel 15 dial
16 stencil

Additional Skill Drill 3 Answers

1 tractor 2 barber 3 catcher 4 anchor 5 pillar
6 beaver 7 scissors 8 drummer 9 grocer 10 collar
11 doctor 12 sculptor 13 quarter 14 dollar 15 armor
16 sailor

6 Finding Eye-Syllables

Short words seem easier to spell than long words. But long words can be divided into short syllables. Then these syllables can be spelled as if they were little words.

First learn to *see* the word parts, or eye-syllables. You can *syllabicate* the long words, as you syllabicated the compounds. Think of the vowel sounds in the word. In most two-syllable words one syllable is louder, or stressed, and you will hear its vowel sound clearly. The other syllable may be soft and have only the soft /ə/ vowel sound.

In some words, however, you can clearly *hear* the vowel sound in the soft syllable, as in the compounds. In such words, spell first one syllable, then the other, as if they were two little words. These syllables have the same spelling options as the one-syllable words.

The VC/CV Eye-Syllables

One of the common spelling patterns in two-syllable English words is this order of letters: one vowel, two consonants, and another vowel—the VCCV order. One way to syllabicate a word in this VCCV pattern is to divide the word between the consonant letters in order to make eye-syllables.

VC|CV	eye-syllables	ear-syllables
dic|tate	dic tate	/dik′ tāt/

VC|CV	eye-syllables	ear-syllables
en|joy	en joy	/en joi′/

In these words you can *hear* the vowel sounds clearly in *both* the stressed syllable and the unstressed syllable. Study the eye-syllable spellings in this chart of VC/CV words. The spelling options for one-syllable words appear again in both the syllables. The first syllables end with a consonant letter, and so their vowel sound is usually short, as in the short-vowel one-syllable words. What are the spelling options for these vowel sounds?

Vowel Spelling Option, First Syllable	Eye-Syllables	Ear-Syllables	Vowel Spelling Option, Second Syllable
___1___ spells /i/	dic tate	/dik′ tāt/	___2___ spells /ā/
___3___ spells /e/	es say	/es′ ā/	___4___ spells /ā/
___5___ spells /ėr/	mer maid	/mėr′ mād/	___6___ spells /ā/
___7___ spells /ô/	cof fee	/kôf′ ē/	___8___ spells /ē/
___9___ spells /o/	pos se	/pos′ ē/	final ___10___ spells /ē/
___11___ spells /a/	stam pede	/stam pēd′/	___12___ spells /ē/
___13___ spells /i/	mis lead	/mis lēd′/	___14___ spells /ē/
___15___ spells /u/	um pire	/um′ pīr/	___16___ spells /ī/
___17___ spells /a/	mag pie	/mag′ pī/	___18___ spells /ī/
___19___ spells /i/	in sight	/in′ sīt/	___20___ spells /ī/
___21___ spells /o/	mot to	/mot′ ō/	final ___22___ spells /ō/
___23___ spells /e/	en fold	/en fōld′/	___24___ spells /ō/
___25___ spells /i/	in road	/in′ rōd/	___26___ spells /ō/
___27___ spells /ėr/	fur row	/fėr′ ō/	___28___ spells /ō/
___29___ spells /i/	im pose	/im pōz′/	___30___ spells /ō/
___31___ spells /e/	res cue	/res′ kū/	___32___ spells /ū/
___33___ spells /o/	cos tume	/kos′ tūm/	___34___ spells /ū/ or /ü/
___35___ spells /i/	mil dew	/mil′ dū/	___36___ spells /ū/ or /ü/
___37___ spells /är/	har poon	/här pün′/	___38___ spells /ü/
___39___ spells /är/	par took	/pär tu̇k′/	___40___ spells /u̇/

Vowel Spelling Option, First Syllable	Eye-Syllables	Ear-Syllables	Vowel Spelling Option, Second Syllable
41 spells /ėr/	sir loin	/sėr′ loin/	42 spells /oi/
43 spells /e/	en joy	/en joi′/	44 spells /oi/
45 spells /e/	en dow	/en dou′/	46 spells /ou/
47 spells /ou/	coun ty	/koun′ tē/	final 48 spells /ē/
49 spells /ô/	aug ment	/ôg ment′/	50 spells /e/
51 spells /ô/	on ward	/ôn′ wərd/	52 spells /ə/
53 spells /i/	pit fall	/pit′ fôl/	54 spells /ô/
55 spells /ãr/	fair ly	/fãr′ lē/	final 56 spells /ē/
57 spells /e/	wel fare	/wel′ fãr/	58 spells /ãr/
59 spells /i/	ig nore	/ig nôr′/	60 spells /ôr/
61 spells /u/	up roar	/up′ rôr′/	62 spells /ôr/
63 spells /i/	sin cere	/sin sir′/	64 spells /ir/
65 spells /ir/	near ly	/nir′ lē/	final 66 spells /ē/

Skill Drill 1 Write the VC/CV words in the chart. After each word write the spelling for the vowel sound in each syllable.

Skill Drill 2 Print the VCCV words. Show the eye-syllables as they are shown in the chart. Look up the meaning of any words you do not know.

1 /mān tān′/	**11** /en′ voi/	**21** /el′ bō/
2 /es′ ā/	**12** /tėr′ mīt/	**22** /ôn′ wərd/
3 /dis′ kount/	**13** /kär tün′/	**23** /nir′ lē/
4 /ig nīt′/	**14** /im pãr′/	**24** /här pün′/
5 /kär′ gō/	**15** /ôr′ bit/	**25** /res′ kū/
6 /kėr′ fū/	**16** /ad hir′/	**26** /um′ pīr/
7 /im pēch′/	**17** /tėr′ moil/	**27** /stam pēd′/
8 /in hāl′/	**18** /hėr′ mit/	**28** /up′ rôr′/
9 /sham pü′/	**19** /in dēd′/	**29** /kôf′ ē/
10 /fôr su̇k′/	**20** /är′ gū/	**30** /im pōz′/

B

Harder VC/CV Words: The /ə/ Syllables

In the words in Skill Drill 2, the vowel sounds can be heard in the soft, or unstressed, syllable as well as in the loud, or stressed, syllable. In most two-syllable words, though, the vowel sound in the soft syllable is not clear. The dictionary usually shows the soft vowel sound as a schwa (/ə/) in the ear-syllable. So you do not get a clear cue to the spelling of the vowel sound in the soft syllable.

But you can find a vowel spelling cue for the soft syllable: Think of the soft syllable as a little word. When you see the word, divide the word into eye-syllables. Say each syllable to yourself as if it were a little word. When you do, you will hear a clear vowel sound in both syllables. Look carefully to see which spelling option is used for the clear vowel sounds and consonant sounds. In the VC/CV words, the vowel sounds are usually short. Remembering the eye-syllables will help you spell the word.

VC | CV
van | dal /van′ dəl/
An *a* spells /ə/. *Think* /van/ and /dal/.

VC | CV
cur | rent /kėr′ ənt/
An *e* spells /ə/. *Think* /kėr/ and /rent/.

VC | CV
vic | tim /vik′ təm/
An *i* spells /ə/. *Think* /vik/ and /tim/.

VC | CV
cus | tom /kus′ təm/
An *o* spells /ə/. *Think* /kus/ and /tom/.

VC | CV
cen | sus /sen′ səs/
A *u* spells /ə/. *Think* /sen/ and /sus/.

Skill Drill 3 Print the regular spellings of these VC/CV words. Mark the eye-syllables. Be sure you know the meanings of all the words. All of them are in the Spelling Dictionary. Check your answers.

1 /tres′ pəs/
2 /sėr′ fəs/
3 /ran′ səm/
4 /pər sü′/
5 /ə fens′/
6 /kə laps′/
7 /sėr′ pənt/
8 /fėr′ təl/
9 /ef′ ərt/
10 /kə līd′/
11 /kap′ səl/
12 /ə nouns′/
13 /kan′ vəs/
14 /ə pēl′/
15 /bėr′ dən/
16 /ə point′/
17 /bliz′ ərd/
18 /här′ vəst/
19 /en′ jən/
20 /stub′ ərn/
21 /prob′ ləm/
22 /en joi′/

The V/CCV and VCC/V Words

Although most VCCV words conveniently divide between the consonant letters, there are some that do not. Some separate as V/CCV and some separate as VCC/V. If you can read the words, you will be able to tell where the division can be made. Then look at the syllables carefully to see which spelling options are used.

In V/CCV words the vowel that ends the first syllable is normally a long vowel, as in one-syllable words like *me* and *so*.

If there is a long vowel sound in the first syllable, mark the eye-syllables V/CCV.

V|CCV
se|cret /sē′ krət/ *Think* /sē/ and /kret/.
a|pron /ā′ prən/ *Think* /ā/ and /pron/.

If there is a two-letter consonant sound, keep the two letters together in the eye-syllables.

th spells /th/
meth|od /meth′ əd/ *Think* /meth/ and /od/.

If you see a familiar word, you probably can mark the eye-syllables to keep the word in one part.

ck spells /k/

rock et /rok′ ət/ *Think* /rok/ and /et/.

VCC|V

count er /koun′ tər/ *Think* /kount/ and /ėr/.

The eye- and ear-syllables need not agree.

Skill Drill 4 Print the spellings for these V/CCV and VCC/V words. Use the examples to help you find the eye-syllables and mark them. Be sure you know the meaning of each word. Look up the meaning of any word you do not know. You will find most words in the Spelling Dictionary at the back of the book. Check your answers.

1 /prō′ gram/
2 /blok ād′/
3 /ē′ stərn/
4 /wiᴛʜ′ ər/
5 /mā′ trən/
6 /vī′ brāt/
7 /ə grē′/
8 /ā′ prən/
9 /blingk′ ər/
10 /fôl′ tē/
11 /fôr′ məl/
12 /mī′ grāt/

Dividing VCCCV Words into Syllables

There are also words that have a VCCCV spelling pattern. The eye-syllables may divide VC/CCV or VCC/CV, depending on whether the middle consonant blends better with the consonant before it or after it.

VC|CCV

hun dred /hun′ drəd/

The *d* and *r* blend better than *n* and *d*. *Think* /hun/ and /dred/.

VCC|CV

sand wich /sand′ wich/

The *n* and *d* blend better than *d* and *w*. *Think* /sand/ and /wich/.

Skill Drill 5 Print these VCCCV words. Find the consonants that blend better and mark the eye-syllables. If you are not sure of a word meaning, check it in the Spelling Dictionary. Check your answers.

1 hamster	**5** handsome	**9** perspire
2 merchant	**6** employ	**10** mattress
3 chuckle	**7** purchase	**11** foundry
4 attract	**8** applaud	**12** sparkle

Dividing VCV Words into Syllables

Many two-syllable words are spelled in the VCV spelling pattern. Many of these words divide *before* the middle consonant letter, that is, into V/CV. When they do, the first syllable ends with a vowel letter. You expect this vowel letter to spell the long vowel sound, as it does in one-syllable words like *me, hi,* and *so.* But almost as many VCV words divide *after* the middle consonant letter, that is, into VC/V. When they do, the first eye-syllable ends with a consonant letter. Then you expect a single vowel before it to spell the short vowel sound, as it does in one-syllable words.

Usually you will hear the vowel sound in the stressed syllable and get a spelling cue. Usually the vowel sound in the unstressed syllable will be /ə/, which will *not* give you a spelling cue. In both V/CV and VC/V words, think of both syllables as little words. Always look carefully at the syllables to see which spelling option is used. Remembering the eye-syllables will restore the spelling cue to the soft syllable.

Study the examples below. Notice where the eye-syllables divide.

V|CV
va|cant /vā′ kənt/

The final *a* in the stressed syllable spells /ā/. The *a* spells /ə/ in the unstressed second syllable. *Think* /vā/ and /kant/. The eye-syllables divide *before* the consonant.

VC|V
mod|est /mod′ əst/

The *o* spells /o/ in the stressed syllable. The *e* spells /ə/ in the unstressed second syllable. *Think* /mod/ and /est/. The eye-syllables divide *after* the consonant.

Skill Drill 6 Print the regular spellings for these VCV words. Mark the eye-syllables. Check the meaning of any word you do not know. Use your Spelling Dictionary. Check your answers.

1 /nō′ mad/	**7** /sə lüt′/	**13** /tī′ rənt/
2 /pan′ ik/	**8** /klī′ mət/	**14** /dē′ sənt/
3 /slō′ gən/	**9** /frē′ kwənt/	**15** /maj′ ik/
4 /sat′ ən/	**10** /val′ ū/	**16** /ten′ ənt/
5 /də lüt′/	**11** /kwī′ nīn/	**17** /pat′ ənt/
6 /tim′ id/	**12** /frā′ grənt/	**18** /siv′ ik/

Blurred Soft Syllables

Several word endings have the same spellings in stressed and in unstressed syllables. In these you can hear the vowel sounds clearly when the syllables are stressed, and then the vowel spellings are easy. But when the syllables are *not* stressed, the vowel sounds are softened and blurred so that the spelling cues disappear. Think of the unstressed syllables as if they were little words in order to remember the spellings more easily.

	Stressed Syllables	Unstressed Syllables
1 en gage /en gāj′/	*age* spells /āj/	
cab bage /kab′ ij/		*age* spells /ij/
ga rage /gə räzh′/	*age* spells /äzh/	

	Stressed Syllables	Unstressed Syllables
2 ar rive /ə rīv′/	*ive* spells /īv/	
ac tive /ak′ tiv/		*ive* spells /iv/
3 con tain /kən tān′/	*ain* spells /ān/	
cap tain /kap′ tən/		*ain* spells /ən/
4 ma ture /mə chu̇r′/	*ture* spells /chu̇r/	
cap ture /kap′ chər/		*ture* spells /chər/
5 as sure /ə shu̇r′/	*sure* spells /shu̇r/	
meas ure /mezh′ ər/		*sure* spells /zhər/
6 dis grace /dis grās′/	*ace* spells /ās/	
pal ace /pal′ əs/		*ace* spells /əs/
7 ad vice /ad vīs′/	*ice* spells /īs/	
no tice /nō′ tis/		*ice* spells /is/

Skill Drill 7 Write the spellings for these words. Be sure you know the meaning of each word. All the words are in the Spelling Dictionary. Check your answers.

1 /sėr′ fəs/	**4** /mə säzh′/	**7** /mə räzh′/
2 /frak′ chər/	**5** /lek′ chər/	**8** /sav′ ij/
3 /mas′ iv/	**6** /nā′ tiv/	**9** /mō′ tiv/

10 /vil′ ən/	**17** /im′ ij/	**24** /kot′ ij/
11 /pas′ chər/	**18** /men′ əs/	**25** /lang′ gwij/
12 /sėr′ vis/	**19** /bär′ gən/	**26** /mes′ ij/
13 /lē′ zhər/	**20** /plezh′ ər/	**27** /voi′ ij/
14 /fėr′ tiv/	**21** /bag′ ij/	**28** /nā′ chər/
15 /rum′ ij/	**22** /sėr′ tən/	**29** /tôr′ chər/
16 /ven′ chər/	**23** /ôf′ is/	**30** /fū′ chər/

Dividing V/V Words

Most English words have VCCV and VCV spelling patterns and are syllabicated before, between, or after the consonants. But some words are syllabicated between vowel letters. Usually the two vowel letters do not spell long vowel sounds as do *ai, ay, ee,* and *oa.* Nor do they spell vowel sounds that *oo, oi, oy, au,* and *aw* spell. Here are some of the V/V words. The V/V words often have three ear-syllables.

V|V
i|*o*

li on /lī′ ən/
vi o lin /vī′ ə lin′/
pi o neer /pī′ ə nir′/
i o dine /ī′ ə dīn/
vi o let /vī′ ə lət/
or i ole /ôr′ ē ōl/

stu di o /stü′ dē ō/
pat i o /pat′ ē ō/
ra ti o /rā′ shē ō/
per i od /pir′ ē əd/
id i ot /id′ ē ət/

V|V
i|*a*

bri ar /brī′ ər/
li ar /lī′ ər/
di al /dī′ əl/
tri al /trī′ əl/
ser i al /sir′ ē əl/
jo vi al /jō′ vē əl/
triv i al /triv′ ē əl/

di a log /dī′ ə lôg/
di a lect /dī′ ə lekt/
di a mond /dī′ ə mənd/
pi an o /pē an′ ō/
ra di ate /rā′ dē āt/
me di ate /mē′ dē āt/

Skill Drill 8 Write the missing *io* and *ia* words. Check your answers.

1 The /rī′ ət/ __ was reported on the /rā′ dē ō/ __.

2 Claudia drew a /dī′ ə gram/ __ in her /dī′ ər ē/ __ today.

V | V
i | *u*

ra di us /rā′ dē əs/	ra di um /rā′ dē əm/
ge ni us /jē′ nē əs/	cal ci um /kal′ sē əm/
me di um /mē′ dē əm/	o pi um /ō′ pē əm/
po di um /pō′ dē əm/	so di um /sō′ dē əm/

V | V
u | *e*

fu el /fū′ əl/	du et /dü et′/
du el /dü′ əl/	su et /sü′ ət/
cru el /krü′ əl/	flu ent /flü′ ənt/

Skill Drill 9 Write the missing *iu* and *ue* words. Check your answers.

1 The /hē′ lē əm/ __ balloon sailed over the /stā′ dē əm/ __.

2 Coal is a good /fū′ əl __.

V|V
u|a

du al /dü′ əl/
u su al /ū′ zhü əl/
ca su al /kazh′ ü əl/
punc tu al /pungk′ chü əl/

grad u al /graj′ ü əl/
vis u al /vizh′ ü əl/

V|V
i|e

di et /dī′ ət/
pi e ty /pī′ ə tē/
sci ence /sī′ əns/
or i ent /ôr′ ē ənt/

pli ers /plī′ ərz/
fi er y /fī′ ər ē/
bar ri er /bar′ ē ər/
car ri er /kar′ ē ər/

Skill Drill 10 Write the missing *ua* and *ie* words.

1 She spoke /kwī′ ət lē/ __ with her new /klī′ ənt/ __ about the case.

2 Diego made his /an′ ū əl/ __ visit to the zoo.

V|V
e|a

i de a /ī dē′ ə/
re al /rē′ əl/
i de al /ī dē′ əl/

ar e a /ãr′ ē ə/
cre ate /krē āt′/
cer e al /sir′ ē əl/

Other V/V

flu id /flü′ id/
gen u ine /jen′ ū ən/
me te or /mē′ tē ər/
ro de o /rō dā′ ō/
the or y /thē′ ər ē/

po et /pō′ ət/
o a sis /ō ā′ sis/
vac u um /vak′ ū əm/
tri umph /trī′ umf/
nu cle us /nü′ klē əs/

Skill Drill 11 Write the missing *ea* and other V/V words. Check your answers.

1 There are /nē′ on/ __ lights over the /mū zē′ əm/ __ downtown.

2 We plan to go to the /thē′ ə tər/ __ tonight.

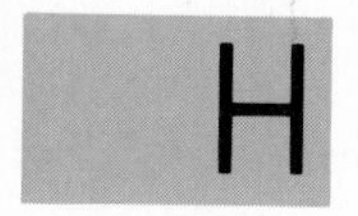

Adding Soft Syllable Endings

Chapter 5 presented these soft-ending spelling options for two-syllable words. The spelling options for soft /ē/ endings, for soft /əl/ endings, and for /ər/ endings are given here.

y and *ey* spell /ē/

emp ty /emp′ tē/ chim ney /chim′ nē/

le, el, al, ol, il, ile, and *ul* spell /əl/

ta ble /tā′ bəl/ lev el /lev′ əl/ rī val /rī′ vəl/
pu pil /pū′ pəl/ i dol /ī′ dəl/ rep tile /rep′ təl/
con sul /kon′ səl/

er, or, and *ar* spell /ər/

bet ter /bet′ ər/ col or /kul′ ər/ col lar /kol′ ər/

These soft syllable endings appear also at the end of three-syllable words. Study these words. Notice the eye-syllables and the ear-syllables.

y *ey*

mel o dy /mel′ ə dē/ at tor ney /ə tėr′ nē/

le	*el*	*al*
ex am ple	sen tin el	car niv al
/eg zam′ pəl/	/sen′ tə nəl/	/kär′ nə vəl/
ter ri ble		prac ti cal
/ter′ ə bəl/		/prak′ tə kəl/

ol	*ile*
cap i tol	ju ven ile
/kap′ ə təl/	/jü′ və nəl/

er	*ar*	*or*
car pen ter	vin e gar	ed it or
/kär′ pən tər/	/vin′ ə gər/	/ed′ ə tər/
cu cum ber	pop u lar	sen a tor
/kū′ kum bər/	/pop′ ū lər/	/sen′ ə tər/

Also, in many *y*-ending verbs, the final *y* spells /ī/.

sat is fy	oc cu py	no ti fy
/sat′ əs fī/	/o′ kū pī/	/nō′ tə fī/
dig ni fy	hor ri fy	jus ti fy
/dig′ nə fī/	/hôr′ ə fī/	/jus′ tə fī/

Look carefully at words with *able* and *ible* suffix endings. Both are pronounced /ə bəl/. Note which spelling option is used, *able* or *ible*.

hor rib le	prob a ble	suit a ble
/hôr′ ə bəl/	/prob′ ə bəl/	/sü′ tə bəl/

Some three-syllable words have a stressed syllable and *two* soft endings. Look carefully to see which soft-syllable spelling option is used in each syllable. Spell the three syllables as if they were little words.

em per or	fed er al	cor por al
/em′ pər ər/	/fed′ ər əl/	/kôr′ pər əl/
bound ar y	jew el ry	mer cur y
/boun′ dər ē/	/jü′ əl rē/	/mėr′ kūr ē/

Skill Drill 12 Read these sound-spellings for soft-ending words. Write the singular and plural noun forms of each word. Look up the meaning of any word you do not know. All the words are in the Spelling Dictionary. Check your answers at the end of Chapter 6.

1 /pol′ ə sē/	**5** /kav′ ə tē/	**9** /fak′ əl tē/
2 /rem′ ə dē/	**6** /bal′ kə nē/	**10** /kom′ ə dē/
3 /sim′ pə thē/	**7** /kum′ pə nē/	**11** /mel′ ə dē/
4 /ā′ jən sē/	**8** /in′ kwər ē/	**12** /ə tėr′ nē/

Skill Drill 13 Read these sound-spellings. Write the present and past tense verb forms of these words. Check your answers at the end of Chapter 6.

1 /tes′ tə fī/	**3** /kwol′ ə fī/	**5** /jus′ tə fī/
2 /sim′ plə fī/	**4** /nō′ tə fī/	**6** /o′ kū pī/

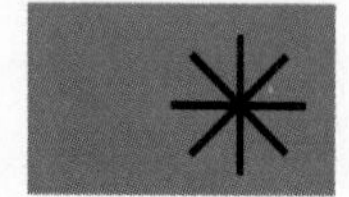

Skill Drill 14 Read these sound-spellings. Write the regular spellings of the words. Check your answers at the end of Chapter 6.

1 /mem′ ər ē/	**5** /his′ tər ē/	**9** /är′ tər ē/
2 /pen′ əl tē/	**6** /loi′ əl tē/	**10** /sē′ nər ē/
3 /sėr′ jər ē/	**7** /sel′ ər ē/	**11** /pol′ ə sē/
4 /lī′ brãr ē/	**8** /bėr′ glər ē/	**12** /kum′ pə nē/

Skill Drill 15 Write these /ər/-ending words. The words are in the Spelling Dictionary. Look up any word you do not know. Check your answers.

1 /tran zis′ tər/	**4** /kon′ trak tər/	**7** /man′ ə jər/
2 /mon′ ə tər/	**5** /spek′ tā tər/	**8** /reg′ ū lər/
3 /sėr′ kū lər/	**6** /sing′ gū lər/	**9** /kən tān′ ər/

Skill Drill 16 Write these /əl/-ending words. Check your answers.

1 /bī′ sik′ əl/	**4** /kom′ ə kəl/	**7** /di sī′ pəl/
2 /sen′ tə nəl/	**5** /vėr′ tik əl/	**8** /krim′ ən əl/
3 /ə rīv′ əl/	**6** /jü′ və nəl/	**9** /pėr′ sə nəl/

Skill Drill 17 Write these *able-* and *ible-*ending words. Check the meaning of any word you do not know. Check your answers.

1 /pos′ ə bəl/	**4** /ô′ də bəl/	**7** /důr′ ə bəl/
2 /süt′ ə bəl/	**5** /flek′ sə bəl/	**8** /ter′ ə bəl/
3 /kā′ pə bəl/	**6** /lī′ kə bəl/	**9** /lej′ ə bəl/

Summary

Long words are easier to spell if they are broken into eye-syllables that can be spelled with the same spelling options as one-syllable words.

1 For vowel-consonant-consonant-vowel words (VCCV words):

- Divide between the consonant letters, as in pen cil (VC/CV).
- Divide before the first consonant letter, as in vi brate (V/CCV).
- Divide after the two consonant letters, as in rath er (VCC/V).

2 For vowel-consonant-consonant-consonant-vowel words (VCCCV words):

- Divide after the first consonant letter, as in ham ster (VC/CCV).
- Divide after the second consonant letter, as in sand wich (VCC/CV).

3 For vowel-consonant-vowel words (VCV words):

- Divide before the consonant letter, as in mu sic (V/CV).
- Divide after the consonant letter, as in com et (VC/V).

4 For two-syllable or three-syllable words with two vowel sounds together (V/V):

- Divide between the vowel letters, as in ri ot and mu se um (V/V).

Long words with soft syllable endings (/ē/, /əl/, /ər/) are easier to learn to spell if you look at the ending to see which spelling option is used. Divide the word into eye-syllables. *Think* of each stressed *and* unstressed syllable as if it were a one-syllable word. When you spell these words, you can use the same spelling options as for one-syllable words.

Learn to look for eye-syllables in words that have soft syllable endings. Then remember the eye-syllables when you spell the words.

Mastery Test 6

Print and mark the eye-syllables of each word.

1 igloo
2 gather
3 perhaps
4 bacon
5 orphan
6 menu
7 destroy
8 cracker
9 canvas
10 banjo
11 betray
12 surplus
13 plastic
14 macron
15 duet
16 blanket
17 athlete
18 stampede
19 riot
20 wagon
21 human
22 comic
23 science
24 donate
25 supreme
26 sandwich
27 recent
28 fuel
29 eclipse
30 relish
31 erase
32 spinach
33 real
34 handsome
35 turnip

Write the correct spelling for each word shown in sound-spelling.

1 An /ə tėr′ nē/ __ for the /kum′ pə nē/ __ /nō′ tə fīd/ __ us of a change in /pol′ ə sē/ __.

2 In my /mem′ ə rē/ __ there has /nev′ ər/ __ been a /bėr′ glər ē/ __ at this /lī′ brãr ē/ __.

3 That /pop′ ū lər/ __ /sen′ ə tər/ __ was once the /reg′ ū lər/ __ /man′ ə jər/ __ at this store.

4 It's not /prak′ tə kəl/ __ for two /sen′ tə nəls/ __ to ride /bī′ sik′ əlz/ __ in the park.

5 Is it /pos′ ə bəl/ __ to make your /ter′ ə bəl/ __ writing more /lej′ ə bəl/ __?

6 The /kraf′ tē/ __ /kôr′ pər əl/ __ stole /jü′ əl rē/ __ from the /em′ pər ər/ __.

7 The /guv′ ər nərz/ __ /pėr′ sən əl/ __ /kär′ pən tərz/ __ are doing /mā′ jər/ __ work on the dome of the /kap′ ə təl/ __.

8 /färm′ ərz/ __ try to /sə plī′/ __ the /kwon′ tə tē/ __ and /kwol′ ə tē/ __ of /sel′ ə rē/ __ the /hung′ grē/ __ men want.

9 This /pak′ ij/ __ /kən tānz′/ __ /mas′ əv/ __ /pik′ chərz/ __ for the /kap′ tənz/ __ /ô′ fəs/ __.

10 The /pal′ əs/ __ /fėr′ nəs/ __ should be /rē plāst′/ __ or I /ven′ chər/ __ to say that the queen will /kəm plān′/ __.

11 My /ad vīs′/ __ is to /mezh′ ər/ __ the wall /sėr′ fəs/ __ before you buy paint for the /gə räzh′/ __.

12 There are /sev′ ə rəl/ __ /eg zam′ pəlz/ __ of /jü′ və nəl/ __ /stôr′ ēz/ __ in books in the /mid′ əl/ __ of the /tā′ bəl/ __ in the library.

Additional Skill Drills

Do these skill drills if you want to improve your Mastery Test score.

Additional Skill Drill 1 Print the VC/CV picture words and mark the eye-syllables. Check your answers.

Additional Skill Drill 2 Print the VCV words and mark the eye-syllables. Check your answers.

Additional Skill Drill 3 Write the spellings for these picture words. Check your answers.

Additional Skill Drill 4 Print the V/V picture words. Use the charts in Section G to mark the eye-syllables. Check your answers.

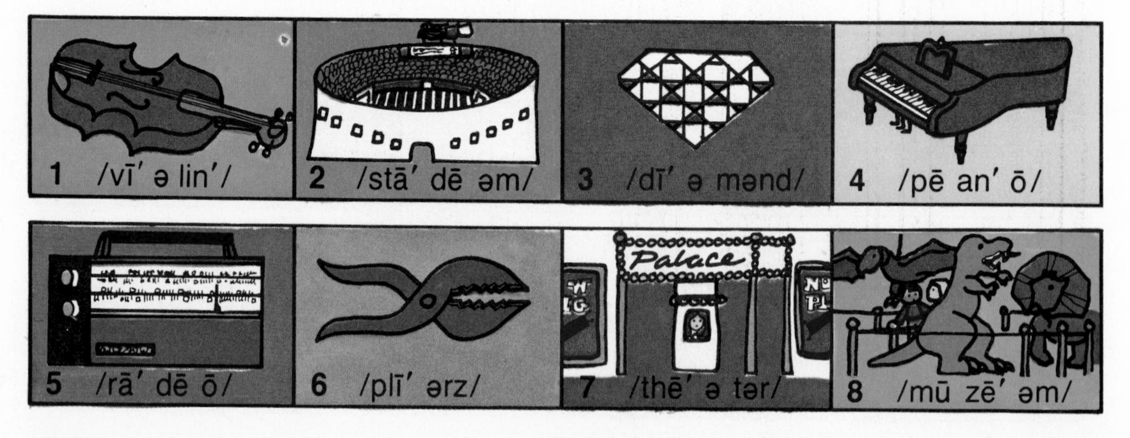

JUNE 7
JUNE 8
9 /dī′ ər ē/
10 /mē′ tē ər/
11 /dī′ əl/
12 /ō ā′ sis/
13 /rō dā′ ō/
14 /sir′ ē əl/
15 /dü et′/
16 /stü′ dē ō/
17 /pō′ et/
18 /vak′ ū əm/
19 /vī′ ə lət/
20 /rā′ dē əs/

Answers for Chapter 6 Skill Drills

Skill Drill 1 Answers

dictate: 1 *i*, 2 *a*-consonant-*e*
essay: 3 *e*, 4 *ay*
mermaid: 5 *er*, 6 *ai*
coffee: 7 *o*, 8 *ee*
posse: 9 *o*, 10 *e*
stampede: 11 *a*, 12 *e*-consonant-*e*
mislead: 13 *i*, 14 *ea*
umpire: 15 *u*, 16 *i*-consonant-*e*
magpie: 17 *a*, 18 *ie*
insight: 19 *i*, 20 *igh*
motto: 21 *o*, 22 *o*
enfold: 23 *e*, 24 *o(ld)*
inroad: 25 *i*, 26 *oa*
furrow: 27 *ur*, 28 *ow*
impose: 29 *i*, 30 *o*-consonant-*e*
rescue: 31 *e*, 32 *ue*
costume: 33 *o*, 34 *u*-consonant-*e*
mildew: 35 *i*, 36 *ew*
harpoon: 37 *ar*, 38 *oo*
partook: 39 *ar*, 40 *oo*
sirloin: 41 *ir*, 42 *oi*
enjoy: 43 *e*, 44 *oy*
endow: 45 *e*, 46 *ow*
county: 47 *ou*, 48 *y*
augment: 49 *au*, 50 *e*
onward: 51 *o*, 52 *a*
pitfall: 53 *i*, 54 *a(l)*
fairly: 55 *air*, 56 *y*
welfare: 57 *e*, 58 *are*
ignore: 59 *i*, 60 *ore*
uproar: 61 *u*, 62 *oar*
sincere: 63 *i*, 64 *ere*
nearly: 65 *ear*, 66 *y*

Skill Drill 2 Answers

1 main tain 2 es say 3 dis count 4 ig nite 5 car go
6 cur few 7 im peach 8 in hale 9 sham poo
10 for sook 11 en voy 12 ter mite 13 car toon
14 im pair 15 or bit 16 ad here 17 tur moil 18 her mit
19 in deed 20 ar gue 21 el bow 22 on ward
23 near ly 24 har poon 25 res cue 26 um pire
27 stam pede 28 up roar 29 cof fee 30 im pose

Skill Drill 3 Answers

1 tres pass 2 sur face 3 ran som 4 pur sue
5 of fense 6 col lapse 7 ser pent 8 fer tile 9 ef fort
10 col lide 11 cap sule 12 an nounce 13 can vas
14 ap peal 15 bur den 16 ap point 17 bliz zard
18 har vest 19 en gine 20 stub born 21 prob lem
22 en joy

Skill Drill 4 Answers

1 pro gram 2 block ade 3 east ern *or* ea stern 4 with er
5 ma tron 6 vi brate 7 a gree 8 a pron 9 blink er
10 fault y 11 form al 12 mi grate

Skill Drill 5 Answers

1 ham ster 2 mer chant 3 chuck le 4 at tract
5 hand some 6 em ploy 7 pur chase 8 ap plaud
9 per spire 10 mat tress 11 found ry *or* foun dry
12 spark le *or* spar kle

Skill Drill 6 Answers

1 no mad 2 pan ic 3 slo gan 4 sat in 5 di lute
6 tim id 7 sal ute *or* sa lute 8 cli mate 9 fre quent
10 val ue 11 qui nine 12 fra grant 13 ty rant
14 de cent 15 mag ic 16 ten ant 17 pat ent 18 civ ic

Skill Drill 7 Answers

1 surface 2 fracture 3 massive 4 massage 5 lecture
6 native 7 mirage 8 savage 9 motive 10 villain
11 pasture 12 service 13 leisure 14 furtive 15 rummage
16 venture 17 image 18 menace 19 bargain
20 pleasure 21 baggage 22 certain 23 office 24 cottage

25 language 26 message 27 voyage 28 nature
29 torture 30 future

Skill Drill 8 Answers

1 riot, radio 2 diagram, diary

Skill Drill 9 Answers

1 helium, stadium 2 fuel

Skill Drill 10 Answers

1 quietly, client 2 annual

Skill Drill 11 Answers

1 neon, museum 2 theater

Skill Drill 12 Answers

1 policy, policies 2 remedy, remedies 3 sympathy, sympathies 4 agency, agencies 5 cavity, cavities 6 balcony, balconies 7 company, companies 8 inquiry, inquiries 9 faculty, faculties 10 comedy, comedies 11 melody, melodies 12 attorney, attorneys

Skill Drill 13 Answers

1 testify, testified 2 simplify, simplified 3 qualify, qualified 4 notify, notified 5 justify, justified 6 occupy, occupied

Skill Drill 14 Answers

1 memory 2 penalty 3 surgery 4 library 5 history 6 loyalty 7 celery 8 burglary 9 artery 10 scenery 11 policy 12 company

Skill Drill 15 Answers

1 transistor 2 monitor 3 circular 4 contractor 5 spectator 6 singular 7 manager 8 regular 9 container

Skill Drill 16 Answers

1 bicycle 2 sentinel 3 arrival 4 comical 5 vertical 6 juvenile 7 disciple 8 criminal 9 personal

Skill Drill 17 Answers

1 possible 2 suitable 3 capable 4 audible 5 flexible 6 likable 7 durable 8 terrible 9 legible

Answers for Chapter 6 Additional Skill Drills

Additional Skill Drill 1 Answers

1 bal loon 2 but ton 3 lan tern 4 cac tus 5 fur nace
6 can non 7 ham mock 8 mus tard 9 por poise
10 scaf fold 11 hel met 12 mit ten

Additional Skill Drill 2 Answers

1 pi lot 2 spi der 3 plan et 4 tu ba 5 rad ish
6 trap eze 7 sher iff 8 ti ger 9 lem on 10 cig ar
11 mag ic 12 sal ute *or* sa lute

Additional Skill Drill 3 Answers

1 necklace 2 picture 3 treasure 4 captive 5 package
6 furnace 7 fountain 8 puncture 9 bandage 10 corsage
11 sausage 12 mountain

Additional Skill Drill 4 Answers

1 vi o lin 2 sta di um 3 di a mond 4 pi an o 5 ra di o
6 pli ers 7 the a ter 8 mu se um 9 di ar y
10 me te or 11 di al 12 o a sis 13 ro de o 14 cer e al
15 du et 16 stu di o 17 po et 18 vac u um 19 vi o let
20 ra di us

7 Proofreading

Proofreading is a skill, and like all skills it needs practice. It is not a simple skill, for proofreading can have different purposes. You may, for example, read what you have written to be sure that it makes good sense. When you focus your attention on the content, you may overlook errors in spelling, punctuation, or capitalization. In proofreading for spelling mistakes, you may miss the punctuation errors. To write a perfect paper, you may have to proofread it several times. Proofread once for spelling, once for punctuation, once for capitalization, etc. If you form the proofreading habit, you may become skillful enough to note several different kinds of errors in one reading.

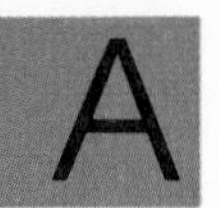

Proofreading One-Syllable Words

Chapter 1 reviewed the spelling options for four kinds of one-syllable words: short-vowel, long-vowel, two-letter vowel, and vowel-*r* words. It reviewed the dictionary sound symbols for twenty-four consonant and eighteen vowel sounds. The spelling options and the sound symbols are summarized in the Spelling and Sound Symbol Chart for One-Syllable Words on pages 13-16.

In this section you will review the spelling options from Chapter 1 by proofreading.

Skill Drill 1 A student wrote the picture-word spellings that follow. Proofread the work for spelling mistakes. Write each of the misspelled words correctly. Check your answers at the end of Chapter 7.

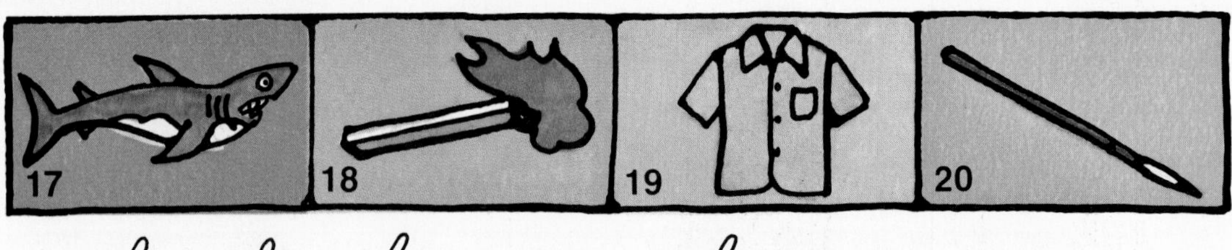

shark bern shirt spear

oar furn square torch

Skill Drill 2 Read the following words and their sound-spellings. The spellings are correct. Proofread the sound-spellings. Write each of the incorrect sound-spellings correctly. Check your answers.

1 stray /strā/
2 bright /brīt/
3 blind /blind/
4 blow /blō/
5 glue /glü/
6 mule /mūl/
7 jail /jāl/
8 ledge /leg/
9 harsh /härsh/
10 curb /kėrb/
11 scare /scär/
12 junk /jungk/
13 whine /hwīn/
14 lock /lok/
15 chew /chue/
16 tax /taks/
17 quilt /kwilt/
18 night /nit/
19 mess /mes/
20 air /ạ̃r/
21 sir /sur/
22 dear /dir/
23 claw /klô/
24 toy /toi/
25 point /point/
26 count /kownt/
27 squirt /skwėrt/
28 sneer /snear/
29 germ /jėrm/
30 star /stär/

Proofreading Silent Consonants and Snurks

Chapter 2 reviewed the silent-consonant spellings. These included *kn* /n/ *(knock)*, *wr* /r/ *(wrong)*, *gn* /n/ *(gnat)*, *mb* /m/ *(comb)*, silent *gh*'s *(night, fright)*, silent *l*'s *(calm, walk)*, *dge* /j/ *(wedge)*, and *tch* /ch/ *(ditch)*. There were also a few others.

Chapter 2 also reviewed a large number of snurks. (Snurks are words that have unexpected spellings.)

Use the word lists in Chapter 2. They will help you complete the proofreading exercises in the skill drills in this section.

Skill Drill 3 Proofread these sentences for silent-consonant spelling mistakes. Write the correct spelling for each misspelled word. Check your answers.

1 I doubt that you would laugh if you caut your thumb in that door lach.

2 I know that beaver gnawed and scratched for hours at that ruff tree limb.

3 He cut his rist with the knife he clutched in the palm of his hand.

4 A crum might lodge in your throat and make you cough.

5 Helga knelt down and rapped a blanket around the lamb and the baby calf.

6 She sied as she listened for one nock that would end her frite.

Skill Drill 4 These sentences include short-vowel snurks from Chapter 2. Some are misspelled. Write each incorrect spelling correctly. Check your answers.

1 We brought them sum bread once a munth.

2 Won of his sons bought some new gloves.

3 None of us ment to shove his way to the front.

4 I guess men of welth dread death as much as anybody else does.

5 I though your young freind ought to build a new trough.

6 Shall we bild a yact to sail in the swomp?

Skill Drill 5 These sentences include long-vowel snurks from Chapter 2. Some are misspelled. Write each incorrect spelling correctly. Check your answers.

1 Even the guide can loose her way leading a group through the fields.

2 The wild colt nayed and tried to break the reins as it bolted away.

3 My neice went to buy a piese of silk to sew on her vail.

4 "You are rogues and thieves!" shrieked the angry priest.

5 The weight of the frate prooved too great to move.

Skill Drill 6 These sentences include snurks that we would expect to spell with two-letter vowel spellings and snurks with vowel-*r* spellings. Some are misspelled. Write each incorrect spelling correctly. Check your answers.

1 Of course they where sure they could learn their new werds.

2 Wet earth should be a good sourse for fishing wormbs.

3 We heard that wolfs were worse scourges than bares.

4 Your perls are worth a lot and should be garded carefully.

5 Our harts leaped when we pushed through the bushes and saw a wolf sitting there.

Proofreading Homonyms

Chapter 3 reviewed homonyms—words that sound the same but that have different meanings and spellings. Homonyms cause many spelling errors. Proofreading for homonym errors is different from proofreading for spelling errors. A homonym may have a correct spelling but a wrong meaning. The following skill drill sentences have no spelling errors. Proofread only to determine whether the correct homonym is being used in each case.

Skill Drill 7 In Chapter 3 the short-vowel homonyms are grouped on pages 56-59 and the long-vowel homonyms on pages 60-71. In the following sentences, find the long- and short-vowel homonyms that are used incorrectly. Then write the homonyms that should have been used instead. Check your answers.

1 We can buy things for a few cents less at the sail.

2 The great pain in his heel and toe made him groan all through the night.

3 The male plain flue strait down to the gait.

4 The whole team will meet on the beech if the son is out.

5 Isabel led the quire down the isle singing a hymn.

6 The prince waved his right to reign on the throne.

7 We peeled the beets and ate them with our stake.

8 Hue down those to yew trees and throw them on the sleigh.

9 The maid found some red aunts in the bread bin.

10 She wants too dye the yolk on her dress a pale blue color.

Skill Drill 8 The two-vowel and vowel-*r* homonyms are grouped on pages 72-76 in Chapter 3. Find the homonyms that are used incorrectly in these sentences. Then write the homonyms that should have been used instead. Check your answers.

1 They do not want to wear there fir coats.

2 Of coarse we want everybody to urn fair pay.

3 The sailors threw their oars in the bow when the boat struck the pier.

4 Two birds sat on a bare bough but the other fowl sored away.

5 The miners used horses to hall the ore from the mine.

6 Their loud coarse voices shouted hoarsely.

7 We used a pair of sheers to cut the chord.

8 The core of scouts set up flares along the route.

9 Phil needed four more boards to finish building the stairs.

10 We could here a hoard of wild horses rush fourth out of the woods.

Proofreading Compounds

Chapter 4 reviewed the spelling of compounds—words made up of two or more smaller words. The little words within a compound were marked off by brackets to show the eye-syllables. You practiced spelling compounds by spelling first one part, then the other part, as if you were spelling two little words.

The compounds are as easy to spell as the little words. One ear-syllable of a compound usually has primary stress and one has secondary stress. The vowel sounds are clear in both syllables. Because this is so, we get spelling cues from the sounds of these words.

The four spelling patterns of one-syllable words appear again in the syllables of the compounds: Some compounds have short-vowel spellings. Some have long-vowel spellings. Some are two-letter vowel spellings. Some have vowel-*r* spellings. A number of the one-syllable snurks also reappear.

If you learned to spell the compounds, you should be able to find the spelling errors in the skill drill sentences that follow. Proofread them to find spelling errors in the compound words only. There are no spelling errors in the other words.

Skill Drill 9 The compounds in these sentences have short- and long-vowel spelling patterns. Find the spelling errors in the compound words. Write the correct spelling for each misspelled word. Check your answers.

1 Armed with shotguns, the officers set up a roadblock.
2 Lifting the heavy sandbags gave me a backake.
3 The livestock is grazing on the hilands.
4 We could see the sunrise from the skylight.
5 We got some beaswax from the beahives.
6 She put her flashlite into her handbag.
7 The little boy let his goldfish swim in the bathtub.
8 We tried to triptoe past the quicksand.
9 Joe tried to hitchike his way by himself.
10 They must have got some soapsuds into these pancakes!

Skill Drill 10 The compounds in these sentences have two-letter vowel spellings and long- and short-vowel spellings. Find the spelling errors in the compound words. Write the correct spelling for each misspelled word. Check your answers.

1 We often play softball on the playground.

2 I always keep a wiskbroom in my suitcase.

3 The cowboys followed the footprints of the outlaws.

4 The snowplow driver had a blowout on the causway.

5 We found a bookcase and some footstools at the pawnchop.

Skill Drill 11 The compounds in these sentences have vowel-*r* spellings as well as other vowel spellings. Find the spelling errors in the compound words. Write the correct spelling for each misspelled word. Check your answers.

1 The crowd burst through the turnstyles and caused an uproar at the ballpark.

2 We couldn't get the whealchair upstares to the storeroom in the wearhouse.

3 We had cornbread and popcorn at the berthday party.

4 The roar of the aircraft at the airport made our eardrums ache.

5 If you can spell *board,* you should spell *scoreboard, switchboard,* and *serfboard* correctly.

Skill Drill 12 The compounds in these sentences include snurk spellings in one of the syllables. Find the spelling errors in the compound words. Write the correct spelling for each misspelled word. Check your answers.

1 News of the earthquake was broadcast over the network.

2 We had hoped to whitewash their team but their touchdown made the game end in a deadlock.

3 Our watchdog surprised a raindear in the cornfield.

4 Anita wiped the windshield with a damp watchcloth.

5 Throughout his childhood their stepsun followed the guidelines his father had given him.

Proofreading Soft Syllable Endings

Chapter 5 reviewed the spellings of two-syllable words with soft-syllable endings. There are three common soft-syllable endings. One is the /ē/ ending, which has the *y* and *ey* spelling options. Another one is the /əl/ ending, which has seven spelling options: *le, el, al, il, ol, ile,* and *ul.* Another one is the /ər/ ending, which is spelled *er, or, ar,* and, in a few words, *ur.*

You also reviewed the rules for spelling /ē/-ending words to which *s, es, ed, er,* and *est* are added: You spell the plural noun form of consonant-*y* words and the *es* verb form of consonant-*y* words by changing *y* to *i* before the *es.* You spell the plural noun form of *ey* words by adding *s.* You spell the *er* and *est* adjective forms of consonant-*y* words and the *ed* verb form of consonant-*y* words by changing the *y* to *i* before adding the ending.

You reviewed the rules for spelling /əl/-ending words to which *ing* is added: Drop the final *e* before adding *ing* to *le* words. Double the final *l* before adding *ing* to vowel-*l* words if the stress is on the last syllable. But do not double the *l* in vowel-*l* words if the stress is not on the last syllable.

Skill Drill 13 Proofread these sentences for spelling errors in /ē/-ending words. Write the correct spelling for each misspelled word. Check your answers.

1 In some countreys the wealthier people live in the cities.

2 People in their twenties and thirties often feel guiltey if they are not busy earning mony.

3 The jockeys hurried to get their entries into the race at the earliest possible time.

4 Juries have often pitied people whose folleys get them into trouble.

5 Greedy men have often envied others who are rewarded for doing their dutey.

6 The dirtyest and noisyest dog in the shop burried its bone under the heaviest papers.

7 The party of wearey travelers rallied to the aid of the lost, hungrey children.

8 I'm dizzey from looking up at that chimny to study those silly turkeys perching there.

Skill Drill 14 Proofread these sentences for spelling errors in /əl/-ending words. Write the correct spelling for each misspelled word. Check your answers.

1 A hostile naval vessel wriggeled safely through the perils of the channel.

2 The owner used a stencil to put a label on the mettle handle of the missile.

3 Some evil vandels broke the fragile idol in the chapel.

4 I scared a squirrel on our picnic table, and the agile rascal ran away.

5 A couple of our pupils thought it futil to learn the formal cymbals for the vowel sounds.

6 Controling the car on this rural gravle path would cause trouble for any mortal driver.

7 The huge diesle rambled through the centrel states toward the less trankwil coastal region.

8 Will you give us a verbal approval for handleing the orul part of the program ourselves?

Skill Drill 15 Proofread these sentences for spelling errors in /ər/-ending words. Write the correct spelling for each misspelled word. Check your answers.

1 The doctor set the collar bone and the broken shoulder of our neighbor's youngster.

2 The buildor used a tractor for the labor of removing bouldars from the storm cellar.

3 The author, a science scholar, had an answer to our question about the soler system.

4 The sculpter used mortar to anchor the piller under her statue.
5 The tailor sewed up his torn sweater for a doller.
6 It would be bettor not to linger when danjer hovers in any manner.
7 Even though he was a miner actor, he conquered the tremar in his voice and spoke with great firvor.
8 The younger scholler shook with laughtor at her father's humor.

Proofreading Longer Words

Chapter 6 reviewed the several ways to divide long words into syllables. When you divide longer words into eye-syllables, you can spell the syllables as you spell one-syllable words. If you "think" stress on each syllable, you will be able to hear the vowel sounds. Then, remembering these eye-syllables, you can use the same spelling options you used in one-syllable words.

A common spelling pattern in two-syllable words is the vowel-consonant-consonant-vowel pattern. We usually syllabicate these words between the two consonant letters to form the eye-syllables. In a vowel–three-consonant–vowel pattern, we may divide after the first consonant letter or after the second one.

Another common pattern is the vowel-consonant-vowel pattern. Sometimes we divide these words before the consonant letter, sometimes after the consonant letter, to form the eye-syllables. A few words have a vowel-vowel pattern in which the two vowels have different sounds. In these words we may divide the eye-syllables between the two vowel letters.

Skill Drill 16 These sentences include words in the VCCV and VCCCV spelling patterns. Proofread the sentences for *any* kind of spelling error. Write the correct spelling for each misspelled word. Check your answers.

1 The fertile soil in our orchard lets us enjoy a fine harvest.

2 The empire ignored our appeals when we tried too argue with him.

3 We agreed not to perchase the house because of the inroads the termites had maid.

4 The stubbern offense of our atholetes collapsed, but we applauded them wildly.

5 The king anounced that he would appoint an envoy to deal formally with foreign problems.

6 If he attempts to impose an unfair curfue, they will ignor his order.

7 Please accept my sinceer wish for your welfare as you persue your new program.

8 How many workers do your merchents employ after the harvest is over?

Skill Drill 17 These sentences include words in the VCV spelling patterns. Proofread the sentences for any kind of spelling error. Write the correct spelling for each misspelled word. Check your answers.

1 The pilot assured the timmid passengers their was no reason for panic.

2 The sherrif's office said it was certain the burgler would be captured.

3 The natives build cottages in the mountains because of the fine climate.

4 The tennant maintained that the fauset in the garage leaked frequently.

5 In the future you will get good service at the bargen counter.

6 Slogans contane special langwage to assure a certain message.

7 I venture to say that it is our nature to expect more time for leesure in the fuchure.

8 The highway serface appeared to be satin, but that image was merely a mirazh.

Skill Drill 18 These sentences include words in which eye-syllables divide between vowel letters. Proofread the sentences for any kind of spelling error. Write the correct spelling for each misspelled word. Check your answers.

1 Manuel turned the radeo dial to here the science lecture.

2 The pupils heard the piano and violin duet in the children's theater.

3 We saw that he had many cashual and even trivial entreys in his diary.

4 A stadium and an art museam will be built in the civic center area.

5 The speakers spoke in there own dialecks but they were as fluent as usual.

6 The acters were puncktual in their arrival at the studeo.

7 She is a genuin geneus to have created such a visual poem!

8 My idea of a real triumf is to break the berrier between us.

Answers to Chapter 7 Skill Drills

Skill Drill 1 Answers

3 gold 6 new 8 snail 10 whale 12 stool 14 crown 18 burn 22 fern

Skill Drill 2 Answers

3 /blīnd/ 8 /lej/ 11 /skãr/ 15 /chü/ *or* /chū/ 18 /nīt/ 21 /sėr/ 26 /kount/ 28 /snir/

Skill Drill 3 Answers

1 caught, latch 2 rough 3 wrist 4 crumb 5 wrapped 6 sighed, knock, fright

Skill Drill 4 Answers

1 some, month 2 One 3 meant 4 wealth 5 thought, friend 6 build, yacht, swamp

Skill Drill 5 Answers

1 lose 2 neighed 3 niece, piece, veil 4 *(No errors)* 5 freight, proved

Skill Drill 6 Answers

1 were, words 2 source, worms 3 wolves, bears 4 pearls, guarded 5 hearts

Skill Drill 7 Answers

1 sale 2 *(No errors)* 3 mail, plane, flew, straight, gate 4 beach, sun 5 choir, aisle 6 waived 7 steak 8 Hew, two 9 ants 10 to, yoke

Skill Drill 8 Answers

1 their, fur 2 course, earn 3 *(No errors)* 4 soared 5 haul 6 *(No errors)* 7 shears, cord 8 corps 9 *(No errors)* 10 hear, horde, forth

Skill Drill 9 Answers

1 *(No errors)* 2 backache 3 highlands 4 *(No errors)* 5 beeswax, beehives 6 flashlight 7 *(No errors)* 8 tiptoe 9 hitchhike 10 *(No errors)*

Skill Drill 10 Answers

1 *(No errors)* 2 whiskbroom 3 *(No errors)* 4 causeway 5 pawnshop

Skill Drill 11 Answers

1 turnstiles 2 wheelchair, upstairs, warehouse 3 birthday 4 *(No errors)* 5 surfboard

Skill Drill 12 Answers

1 *(No errors)* 2 *(No errors)* 3 reindeer 4 washcloth 5 stepson

Skill Drill 13 Answers

1 countries 2 guilty, money 3 *(No errors)* 4 follies 5 duty 6 dirtiest, noisiest, buried 7 weary, hungry 8 dizzy, chimney

Skill Drill 14 Answers

1 wriggled 2 metal 3 vandals 4 *(No errors)* 5 futile, symbols 6 Controlling, gravel 7 diesel, central, tranquil 8 handling, oral

Skill Drill 15 Answers

1 *(No errors)* 2 builder, boulders 3 solar 4 sculptor, pillar 5 dollar 6 better, danger 7 minor, tremor, fervor 8 scholar, laughter

Skill Drill 16 Answers

1 *(No errors)* 2 umpire, to 3 purchase, made 4 stubborn, athletes 5 announced 6 curfew, ignore 7 sincere, pursue 8 merchants

Skill Drill 17 Answers

1 timid, there 2 sheriff's, burglar 3 *(No errors)* 4 tenant, faucet 5 bargain 6 contain, language, 7 leisure, future 8 surface, mirage

Skill Drill 18 Answers

1 radio, hear 2 *(No errors)* 3 casual, entries 4 museum 5 their, dialects 6 actors, punctual, studio 7 genuine, genius 8 triumph, barrier

Guide to the Dictionary

The Spelling Dictionary includes over 500 of the words used in the skill drills of this level or as examples in the study charts. Guide words are given at the top of each page. A pronunciation key is shown at the bottom of every right-hand page.

An entry word is shown in heavy black type.

Pronunciation is shown in sound-symbols between slant lines after each entry word.

• **donor** /dō′ nər/ *n.* Person who gives; giver.

Spaces are used to show where the ear-syllables divide in the sound-spelling of an entry word.

• **flexible** /flek′ sə bəl/ *adj.* Able to be bent without breaking; not stiff.

The primary accent is shown by the darker accent mark.

The secondary accent is shown by the lighter accent mark.

• **flashlight** /flash′ līt′/ *n.* A portable electric light.

The part or parts of speech for an entry word are shown by abbreviations.

• **honor** /on′ ər/ *n.* Glory; fame; good name. —*v.* Respect; think highly of.

A plural of a noun is shown if it does not form the plural regularly by adding *s* or *es* to the singular.

• **oasis** /ō ā′ sis/ *n*. Fertile spot in the desert where there is water. *pl.* **oases.**

The *er* and *est* adjective forms are shown when the spelling of the entry word is changed before the endings are added.

• **spicy** /spī′ sē/ *adj.* **1.** Flavored with spice. **2.** Like spice. **3.** Lively; keen. **spicier, spiciest.**

The past tense and *ing* verb forms are shown if the spelling of the entry word is changed before the endings are added or if the verb is irregular.

• **testify** /tes′ tə fī/ *v.* Give evidence; say as a witness; declare. **testified, testifying.**

• **amaze** /ə māz′/ *v.* To surprise greatly; strike with sudden wonder. **amazed, amazing.**

Words with the same spelling and very different meanings are shown as separate entry words.

• **pupil**[1] /pū′ pəl/ *n.* Person who is learning in school or is being taught by someone.

• **pupil**[2] /pū′ pəl/ *n.* The black center of the eye where light enters.

The authors are indebted to Scott, Foresman and Company for permission to use and adapt definitions from the Thorndike-Barnhart Intermediate Dictionary by E. L. Thorndike and Clarence L. Barnhart.

Spelling Dictionary

- **adhere** /ad hir′/ *v.* Stick fast: *Mud adheres to our shoes; He adheres to his ideas even when they are proved wrong.* **adhered, adhering.**
- **agency** /ā′ jən sē/ *n.* **1.** The office or business of some person or company that acts for another: *An agency rented our house for us.* **2.** Means; action: *Snow is drifted by the agency of the wind. pl.* **agencies.**
- **agile** /aj′ əl/ *adj.* Moving easily and quickly; nimble: *an agile athlete; an agile mind.*
- **alley** /al′ ē/ *n.* **1.** Narrow back street. **2.** A long, narrow, enclosed place for bowling. *pl.* **alleys.**
- **amaze** /ə māz′/ *v.* To surprise greatly; strike with sudden wonder: *She was so amazed by the surprise party that she could not think of a thing to say.* **amazed, amazing.**
- **angel** /ān′ jəl/ *n.* **1.** Messenger for a deity. **2.** Person as good or lovely as an angel.
- **announce** /ə nouns′/ *v.* **1.** To give formal or public notice of. **2.** Make known the presence or arrival of. **announced, announcing.**
- **anvil** /an′ vəl/ *n.* An iron or steel block on which metals are hammered and shaped.
- **appeal** /ə pēl′/ *v.* **1.** Make an earnest request; ask for help. **2.** Be attractive, interesting, or enjoyable: *Piano music appeals to me more than violin music.* –*n.* **1.** An earnest request; a call for help. **2.** Attraction; interest: *Motion pictures have a great appeal for many people.*
- **applaud** /ə plôd′/ *v.* **1.** Show approval by clapping the hands. **2.** Approve; praise: *Father applauded my decision to remain in school.*
- **appoint** /ə point′/ *v.* **1.** Name a person for a position or job; choose. **2.** Decide on; set: *appoint a day for the meeting.*
- **arbor** /är′ bər/ *n.* A shaded place formed by trees or shrubs or by vines growing on a lattice.
- **area** /ãr′ ē ə/ *n.* **1.** Amount of surface: *The area of the floor is 600 square feet.* **2.** Range of interest or knowledge: *Our science teacher is familiar with this area of chemistry.* **3.** Region: *a mountainous area. pl.* **areas.**
- **argue** /är′ gū/ *v.* **1.** Discuss with someone who disagrees. **2.** Try to prove by reasoning. **argued, arguing.**
- **armor** /är′ mər/ *n.* **1.** A covering, usually of metal or leather, worn to protect the body in fighting. **2.** Any kind of protective covering: *The steel plates of a warship and the scales of a fish are armor.*
- **artery** /är′ tər ē/ *n.* **1.** Any of the tubes that carry blood from the heart to all parts of the body. **2.** Main road; important channel: *Broadway is the main artery of traffic in the city. pl.* **arteries.**
- **asphalt** /as′ fôlt/ *n.* **1.** Dark substance much like tar, found in various parts of the world or obtained by refining petroleum. **2.** A mixture of this substance with crushed rock or sand, used in surfacing roads.
- **athlete** /ath′ lēt/ *n.* Person trained in exercise of physical strength, speed, and skill: *Baseball players, runners, boxers, and swimmers are athletes.*
- **attorney** /ə tėr′ nē/ *n.* **1.** One who has the power to act in another's place. **2.** A lawyer. *pl.* **attorneys.**
- **attract** /ə trakt′/ *v.* **1.** Draw to oneself. **2.** Be pleasing to: *Bright colors attract children.*
- **audible** /ô′ də bəl/ *adj.* Able to be heard; loud enough to be heard: *She spoke in such a low voice that her remarks were barely audible.*

b

- **backache** /bak′ āk′/ *n.* Pain in the back.
- **baggage** /bag′ ij/ *n.* Trunks or suitcases taken along in travel.
- **balcony** /bal′ kə nē/ *n.* **1.** Outside projecting platform with an entrance from an upper floor of a building. **2.** Upper floor in a theater or hall with seats for an audience. *pl.* **balconies.**
- **bargain** /bär′ gən/ *n.* **1.** Agreement to trade or exchange. **2.** Something offered for sale cheap: *This hat is a bargain.* –*v.* Try to make a good deal.

• **barley** /bär′ lē/ *n.* A grasslike plant or its grain, growing in a cool climate and used for food.

• **barrel** /bar′ əl/ *n.* **1.** Container with a round, flat top and bottom and sides that curve out slightly. **2.** Amount that a barrel can hold: *a barrel of apples.* **3.** The metal tube of a gun.

• **barrier** /bar′ ē ər/ *n.* **1.** Something standing in the way to prevent progress or approach. **2.** Something that separates and keeps apart.

• **beeswax** /bēz′ waks′/ *n.* Wax given out by bees, from which they make their honeycomb.

• **bellboy** /bel′ boi′/ *n.* Man or boy whose work is carrying baggage and doing errands for guests of a hotel or club.

• **blindfold** /blīnd′ fōld′/ *n.* A cover over the eyes, blocking vision. *–v.* Cover the eyes of.

• **blinker** /blingk′ ər/ *n.* A warning signal with flashing lights.

• **blizzard** /bliz′ ərd/ *n.* A blinding snowstorm with very strong wind and very great cold.

• **blockade** /blok ād′/ *n.* **1.** Control of who or what goes into or out of a place by the use of the army or navy. **2.** Anything that blocks up or obstructs. *–v.* **1.** Put under blockade. **2.** Block up; obstruct. **blockaded, blockading.**

• **blowout** /blō′ out′/ *n.* **1.** The bursting of an automobile tire. **2.** A sudden escape of air, steam, or the like.

• **bluegrass** /blü′ gras′/ *n.* Grass with bluish-green stems, valuable for pasturage and hay.

• **boldface** /bōld′ fās′/ *n.* Type that has thick, heavy lines, used for emphasis. *–adj.* Type set in such type: *boldface words.*

• **bolster** /bōl′ stər/ *v.* Keep from falling; prop; support: *Their sympathy bolstered her courage.* *–n.* Long pillow for a bed.

• **boulder** /bōl′ dər/ *n.* A large rock, rounded or worn by the action of water and weather.

• **briar** /brī′ ər/ *n.* Thorny or prickly plant or bush. (Also spelled *brier.*)

• **broadcast** /brôd′ kast′/ *n.* Message sent out by radio or television; radio or television program. *–v.* **1.** Send out by radio or television. **2.** Scatter widely: *Don't broadcast gossip.*

• **brutal** /brü′ təl/ *adj.* Like a brute; coarse; cruel and savage.

• **bulky** /bul′ kē/ *adj.* **1.** Taking up much space; large: *Bulky shipments are often sent in freight cars.* **2.** Hard to handle; clumsy: *She dropped the bulky package twice.* **bulkier, bulkiest.**

• **bully** /bu̇l′ ē/ *n.* Person who frightens, teases, or hurts others who are not as strong. *pl.* **bullies.** *–v.* Frighten into doing something by noisy talk or threats. **bullied, bullying.**

• **burden** /bėr′ dən/ *n.* **1.** A load; what is carried. **2.** A load too heavy to carry easily: *a burden of debts.* *–v.* Weigh down; load too heavily.

• **bushel** /bu̇sh′ əl/ *n.* **1.** Measure for grain, fruit, vegetables, and other dry things, equal to 4 pecks or 32 quarts. **2.** Container that holds one bushel.

• **bushy** /bu̇sh′ ē/ *adj.* **1.** Like a bush. **2.** Overgrown with bushes. **bushier, bushiest.**

• **busy** /biz′ ē/ *adj.* **1.** Working; active. **2.** In use. **busier, busiest.** *–v.* Make busy; keep busy. **busied, busying.**

C

• **calcium** /kal′ sē əm/ *n.* Substance which is part of limestone, chalk, milk, bone, shells, teeth, and many other things: *You need enough calcium in your food to grow strong, healthy bones.*

• **camel** /kam′ əl/ *n.* Large four-footed mammal with long neck and cushioned feet, used as beast of burden in desert regions. The camel of northern Africa has one hump; the camel of central Asia has two humps.

• **camphor** /kam′ fər/ *n.* White substance with a strong odor and a bitter taste, used to protect clothes from moths.

• **cancel** /kan′ səl/ *v.* **1.** Put an end to; set aside; do away with: *We canceled our order for the books.* **2.** Cross out; mark so that it cannot be used again.

• **canvas** /kan′ vəs/ *n.* **1.** Strong cloth with a coarse weave made of cotton, flax, or hemp, used to make tents, sails, certain articles of clothing, and to paint on. **2.** Something made of canvas: *The artist painted on canvas.* **3.** Picture painted on canvas: *Ten canvases were stolen from the museum.* *pl.* **canvases.** *–adj.* Made of canvas: *canvas sails.*

/a/ ran /ā/ rain /ã/ care /ä/ car /e/ hen /ē/ he /ėr/ her /i/ in /ī/ ice /o/ not /ō/ no /ô/ off /u/ us /ū/ use /ü/ tool /u̇/ took /ou/ cow /oi/ boy /ch/ church /hw/ when /ng/ sing /sh/ ship /ᴛʜ/ this /th/ thin /zh/ vision /ə/ about, taken, pencil, lemon, circus

• **capable** /kā′ pə bəl/ *adj.* Able; having power or ability: *a capable teacher.* **capable of,** having ability, power, or fitness for: *The modern airplane is capable of going 1000 miles an hour.*

• **capsule** /kap′ səl/ *n.* **1.** Small case or covering: *Medicine is often given in capsules made of gelatin.* **2.** The enclosed front section of a rocket made to carry astronauts or instruments into space.

• **captor** /kap′ tər/ *n.* Person who takes and holds a prisoner.

• **cargo** /kär′ gō/ *n.* Load of goods carried by a ship or plane: *to unload a cargo of wheat. pl.* **cargoes** or **cargos.**

• **cartoon** /kär tün′/ *n.* **1.** Sketch or drawing which interests or amuses us by showing persons, events, or things in an exaggerated way. **2.** Comic strip.

• **casual** /kazh′ ü əl/ *adj.* **1.** Happening by chance; not planned. **2.** Careless: *a casual glance at the newspaper.* **3.** Informal: *casual clothes for the picnic.*

• **causeway** /kôz′ wā′/ *n.* **1.** Raised road or path across low, wet ground. **2.** A highway; paved roadway.

• **cavity** /kav′ ə tē/ *n.* Hollow place; hole: *Most cavities in teeth are caused by decay. pl.* **cavities.**

• **cedar** /sē′ dər/ *n.* An evergreen tree with wide spreading branches. Its fragrant, durable, reddish wood is much used for lining clothes closets and making chests, pencils, and posts.

• **celery** /sel′ ər ē/ *n.* Vegetable whose long, crisp stalks are whitened by keeping the stalks covered as they grow. Celery is eaten raw or cooked.

• **cellar** /sel′ ər/ *n.* Underground room or rooms, usually under a building and often used for storing food or fuel.

• **central** /sen′ trəl/ *adj.* **1.** At the center; near the center: *the central part of the city.* **2.** Forming the center: *The sun is central in the solar system.* **3.** Head: *The central library sends books to its branches.* **4.** Equally distant from all points. **5.** Main; chief; principal: *the central idea of the story.*

• **cereal** /sir′ ē əl/ *n.* **1.** Any grass that produces grain used as a food. **2.** The grain of such grass. **3.** Food made from such grain: *Oatmeal is a cereal.* –*adj.* Having something to do with the grain or the grasses producing it. [*Cereal* is derived from the Latin word *Cerealis,* meaning "of the goddess *Ceres,*" the goddess of harvest and agriculture.]

• **certain** /sėr′ tən/ *n.* **1.** Sure. **2.** Some; particular. **3.** Settled: *She earns a certain amount of money each week.* **4.** Reliable.

• **chamber** /chām′ bər/ *n.* **1.** A room, especially a bedroom. **2.** Hall where lawmakers meet: *the council chamber.* **3.** Group of lawmakers: *The Senate is one chamber of the Congress of the United States.* **4.** An enclosed space in the body of an animal or plant or in some kinds of machinery: *the chamber of the heart; the chambers of a gun.*

• **channel** /chan′ əl/ *n.* **1.** Bed of a stream. **2.** Body of water that joins two larger bodies. **3.** Deeper part of a waterway. **4.** Means by which something is carried: *The spy worked through secret channels.* –*v.* Form a channel in. **channeled, channeling.**

• **chapel** /chap′ əl/ *n.* **1.** A building for worship, not as large as a church. **2.** Small place for worship in a larger building: *a hospital chapel.* [*Chapel* is derived from the old French word *capella* meaning "small cape," and the Latin word *cappa,* meaning "cloak." The word *cappa* was applied to a shrine containing the cloak of St. Martin.]

• **charcoal** /chär′ kōl′/ *n.* A black, brittle form of carbon made by partly burning wood or bones in an airtight place: *Charcoal is used as fuel, in filters, and as a pencil for drawing.*

• **childhood** /chīld′ hu̇d′/ *n.* **1.** Condition of being a child. **2.** Time during which one is a child.

• **chisel** /chiz′ əl/ *n.* Tool with a steel cutting edge at the end of a strong blade, used for shaping wood, stone, or metal. –*v.* Cut or shape with a chisel: *The sculptor was at work chiseling a statue.*

• **chuckle** /chuk′ əl/ *v.* Laugh to oneself. **chuckled, chuckling.** –*n.* A soft laugh; quiet laughter.

• **circular** /sėr′ kū lər/ *adj.* **1.** Round like a circle: *The full moon has a circular shape.* **2.** Moving in a circle. –*n.* Letter, notice, or advertisement sent to each of a number of people.

• **civic** /siv′ ik/ *adj.* **1.** Having something to do with a city: *civic buildings; civic affairs.* **2.** Having to do with citizens or citizenship: *civic duties.*

- **civil** /siv′ əl/ *adj.* **1.** Having something to do with citizens: *civil duties.* **2.** Not naval, military, or connected with the church: *a civil court.* **3.** Polite: *a civil answer.*
- **clamor** /klam′ ər/ *n.* **1.** Loud noise, especially of voices; confused shouting. **2.** Noisy demand: *The men made a great clamor for better working conditions.* —*v.* Make a loud noise.
- **cleanser** /klen′ zər/ *n.* Substance that cleans: *Stores today sell many good cleansers for floors and furniture.*
- **client** /klī′ ənt/ *n.* **1.** Person for whom a lawyer acts. **2.** Customer.
- **climate** /klī′ mət/ *n.* **1.** Kind of weather a place has. **2.** Region with certain conditions of heat and cold, rainfall, etc.
- **coastal** /kōst′ əl/ *n.* At, on, or near the coast, or seashore.
- **coffee** /kôf′ ē/ *n.* A dark brown drink made from the roasted and ground seeds of a coffee tree. —*adj.* The color of coffee.
- **collapse** /kə laps′/ *n.* **1.** Fall in; sink together suddenly. **2.** Break down; fail suddenly: *The business collapsed.* **collapsed, collapsing.** —*n.* **1.** Sudden shrinking together. **2.** Breakdown; failure: *a nervous collapse.*
- **collide** /kə līd′/ *v.* **1.** Hit or strike hard together. **2.** Clash; conflict. **collided, colliding.**
- **comedy** /kom′ ə dē/ *n.* **1.** An amusing play that has a happy ending. **2.** A funny happening. *pl.* **comedies.**
- **company** /kum′ pə nē/ *n.* **1.** Group of people. **2.** Group of people joined together for a purpose. **3.** Companions. **4.** Companionship. **5.** Guest or guests. **6.** Part of an army. *pl.* **companies.**
- **condor** /kon′ dər/ *n.* Large vulture with bare neck and head, living in the high mountains of South America and California.
- **conductor** /kən duk′ tər/ *n.* **1.** Guide or leader; person who is conducting. **2.** Person in charge of passengers on a train or a bus. **3.** Substance capable of transmitting heat, electricity, light, or sound.
- **conquer** /kong′ kər/ *v.* Overcome by force; get the better of; take in war.
- **container** /kən tān′ ər/ *n.* Box, can, jar, or carton used to hold something.
- **contractor** /kon′ trak tər/ *or* /kən trak′ tər/ *n.* Person who agrees to furnish materials or to do a piece of work for a certain price: *a building contractor; an electrical contractor.*
- **copy** /kop′ ē/ *n.* **1.** Something made to be just like another. **2.** One of a number of books, magazines, newspapers, or pictures made at the same printing. *pl.* **copies.** —*v.* **1.** Make a copy of. **2.** Be a copy of. **copied, copying.**
- **corridor** /kôr′ ə dər/ *n.* Long hallway; passage in a large building into which rooms open.
- **cottage** /kot′ ij/ *n.* **1.** Small house. **2.** House at a summer resort.
- **cougar** /kü′ gər/ *n.* Puma; mountain lion; tawny North or South American wildcat.
- **countdown** /kount′ doun′/ *n.* **1.** The time just before the launching of a missile or rocket. **2.** The calling out of the passing minutes or seconds of this period as they pass.
- **country** /kun′ trē/ *n.* **1.** Land; region. **2.** All of a nation. **3.** Land where a person is a citizen. **4.** People of a nation. **5.** Land outside of cities and towns. *pl.* **countries.** —*adj.* Of the country.
- **couple** /kup′ əl/ *n.* **1.** Two things of a kind that go together; pair: *a couple of socks.* **2.** Man and woman who are married, engaged, or partners in a dance. —*v.* Join together: *The brakeman coupled the freight cars.* **coupled, coupling.**
- **courtyard** /kôrt′ yärd′/ *n.* Space enclosed by walls, in or near a large building.
- **create** /krē āt′/ *v.* **1.** Make a thing which has not been made before; bring into being: *create a garden in the desert.* **2.** Be the cause of: *create a disturbance.* **created, creating.**
- **cruel** /krü′ əl/ *adj.* **1.** Ready to give pain to others. **2.** Showing a cruel nature: *cruel acts.* **3.** Causing pain or suffering: *a cruel war.*
- **crystal** /kris′ təl/ *n.* **1.** A clear, transparent mineral that looks like ice. **2.** Very transparent glass or plastic over the face of a watch. **3.** One of the regularly shaped pieces with angles and flat surfaces into which many substances solidify. —*adj.* **1.** Made of crystal: *crystal beads.* **2.** Clear and transparent like crystal: *crystal water.*

• **cucumber** /kū' kum bər/ *n.* A long, green vegetable with firm flesh inside.

• **cudgel** /kuj' əl/ *n.* A short, thick stick used as a weapon; club. —*v.* Beat with a cudgel.

• **cupcake** /kup' kāk'/ *n.* A small cake baked in a pan shaped like a cup.

• **curfew** /kėr' fū/ *n.* **1.** Rule requiring that certain persons be off the streets or at home before a fixed time. **2.** Ringing of a bell at a fixed time in the evening as a signal. **3.** Time when a curfew begins.

• **curry** /kėr' ē/ *n.* **1.** A peppery sauce or powder. **2.** Food flavored with curry. *pl.* **curries.** —*v.* Rub and clean (a horse) with a brush or currycomb. **curried, currying.**

d

• **damsel** /dam' səl/ *n.* Maiden; young girl.

• **deadlock** /ded' lok'/ *n.* State in which progress is impossible; complete standstill in a dispute. —*v.* Bring to a deadlock; cause a deadlock, or standstill in a dispute.

• **debtor** /det' ər/ *n.* Person who owes something to another.

• **decent** /dē' sənt/ *adj.* **1.** Proper and right; respectable. **2.** Good enough; not wonderful and not very bad: *a decent excuse.*

• **dental** /den' təl/ *adj.* **1.** Of or for the teeth: *dental care.* **2.** Of or for a dentist's work: *a dental chair.*

• **diagram** /dī' ə gram/ *n.* Drawing or sketch showing the important parts of a thing. —*v.* Put on paper or on the chalkboard in the form of a drawing or sketch; make a diagram of.

• **dial** /dī' əl/ *n.* **1.** A moving surface on which a pointer shows how much there is of something. **2.** Plate or disk of a radio or television set with numbers and letters on it for tuning into a radio or television station. **3.** Part of an automatic telephone used in making telephone calls. —*v.* **1.** Tune in by using a radio or television dial. **2.** Call by means of a telephone dial.

• **dialect** /dī' ə lekt/ *n.* Form of speech spoken in a certain district or by a certain group of people: *There are many dialects of American English.*

• **dialog** /dī' ə lôg/ *n.* **1.** Conversation: *The two actors had a dialog in the middle of the stage.* **2.** Conversation written out: *The book has a good plot and much clever dialog.* (Also spelled *dialogue.*)

• **diary** /dī' ər ē/ *n.* **1.** Account, written down each day, of what has happened to one, or what one has done or thought during the day. **2.** A blank book with a space for each day in which to keep a daily record. *pl.* **diaries.**

• **diesel** /dē' zəl/ *n.* Engine that burns oil ignited by heat caused by the compression of air. [*Diesel* is taken from the name of Rudolf *Diesel,* a German engineer who invented this engine in the 1890's.]

• **diet** /dī' ət/ *n.* **1.** The usual kind of food and drink: *His diet is made up of meat and vegetables.* **2.** Any special foods eaten in sickness or to make oneself fat or thin: *a liquid diet.* —*v.* Eat special food to gain or lose weight. **dieted, dieting.**

• **dilute** /də lüt'/ *v.* Make weaker or thinner by adding water or some other liquid. **diluted, diluting.** —*adj.* Weakened or thinned by the addition of water or some other liquid.

• **disciple** /di sī' pəl/ *n.* **1.** Believer in the thought and teaching of any leader; follower. **2.** One of the followers of Jesus.

• **discount** /dis' kount/ *v.* **1.** Take off a certain amount from a price: *The store discounts 2 per cent on all bills paid when due.* **2.** Believe only a part of: *I discount what he says because he is known to exaggerate stories.* —*n.* Amount taken off from a price: *a discount of 20 per cent.*

• **dismal** /diz' məl/ *adj.* **1.** Dark; gloomy: *a dismal cave.* **2.** Dreary; miserable: *Sickness made the girl feel dismal.*

• **donkey** /dong' kē/ *or* /dông' kē/ *n.* Small animal somewhat like a horse but with longer ears, a shorter mane, and a tuft of hair at the end of its tail. *pl.* **donkeys.**

• **donor** /dō' nər/ *n.* Person who gives; giver: *The rich woman was a generous donor to the public library.*

• **double** /dub' əl/ *adj.* **1.** Twice as much, as large, or as strong. **2.** In a pair: *double consonants.* **3.** Having two meanings or characters. —*n.* **1.** Number or amount that is twice as much. **2.** Person or thing that is just like another. **3.** A fold. —*v.* **1.** Become twice as much. **2.** Fold over. **3.** Turn sharply backward. **doubled, doubling.** —*adv.* Twice: *He was paid double by mistake.*

• **downfall** /doun' fôl'/ *n.* **1.** Bringing to ruin; sudden overthrow: *the downfall of an empire; Pride was his downfall.* **2.** A heavy fall of rain or snow.

• **dowry** /dou' rē/ *n.* **1.** Money or property a woman brings to her husband when she marries him. **2.** A gift of nature; natural talent: *Good health is a useful dowry. pl.* **dowries.**

• **dual** /dü' əl/ *or* /dū' əl/ *adj.* **1.** Consisting of two parts; double: *dual controls of the airplane.* **2.** Showing two.

• **duel** /dü' əl/ *or* /dū' əl/ *n.* **1.** A formal fight to settle a quarrel. **2.** Any contest between opposing parties: *The lawyers fought a duel of words in court.* –*v.* Fight a duel.

• **duet** /dü et'/ *n.* **1.** Piece of music for two voices or instruments. **2.** Two singers or instruments performing together.

• **durable** /dủr' ə bəl/ *adj.* **1.** Able to withstand wear or decay: *durable fabric.* **2.** Lasting a long time: *durable peace between nations.*

• **duty** /dü' tē/ *or* /dū' tē/ *n.* **1.** The thing that is right to do: *a duty to obey rules.* **2.** Obligation: *A sense of duty made him stay home with his sick brother.* **3.** Things a person has to do in his work: *a teacher's duties.* **4.** Tax on articles taken out of or brought into a country. *pl.* **duties.**

e

• **early** /ėr' lē/ *adv., adj.* **1.** In the first part. **2.** Before the usual time. **3.** Soon. **earlier, earliest.**

• **earthquake** /ėrth' kwāk'/ *n.* A shaking or sliding of the ground, caused by the sudden movement of rock beneath the earth's surface.

• **easel** /ē' zəl/ *n.* A stand for a picture or blackboard.

• **edible** /ed' ə bəl/ *adj.* Fit to eat.

• **effort** /ef' ərt/ *n.* **1.** Use of energy and strength to do something: *Climbing a hill takes effort.* **2.** Hard try; strong attempt. **3.** Result of effort: *Works of art are artistic efforts.*

• **eggplant** /eg' plant'/ *n.* Plant with large purple fruit shaped something like an egg, used as a vegetable.

• **eighty** /ā' tē/ *n., adj.* Eight times ten; 80.

• **elbow** /el' bō/ *n.* **1.** Joint between the upper and lower arm. **2.** Any bend or corner having the same shape as a bent arm. –*v.* Push with the elbow.

• **employ** /em ploi'/ *v.* **1.** Give work and pay to: *The hotel employs a cook.* **2.** Use: *You employ a fork in eating.* **3.** Keep busy: *employ yourself in reading.*

• **engine** /en' jən/ *n.* **1.** Machine for applying power to some work. **2.** Machine that pulls a railroad train. **3.** Anything used to bring about a result.

• **enjoy** /en joi'/ *v.* Have or use with joy; be happy with; take pleasure in.

• **entry** /en' trē/ *n.* **1.** Act of entering. **2.** Place or way by which to enter. **3.** Thing written or printed in a book, list, etc.: *the entry words in a dictionary.* **4.** Person or thing that takes part in a contest. *pl.* **entries.**

• **envoy** /en' voi/ *n.* **1.** Messenger. **2.** Diplomat next below an ambassador in rank.

• **envy** /en' vē/ *n.* **1.** Discontent at another's good fortune. **2.** Object of such feeling; person who is envied: *The girl with the new bicycle was the envy of the class. pl.* **envies.** –*v.* **1.** Feel envy toward: *Some people envy the rich.* **2.** Feel envy because of: *He envied his friend's success.* **envied, envying.**

• **equal** /ē' kwəl/ *adj.* The same in amount, size, number, value, or rank. –*v.* **1.** Be the same as. **2.** Make or do something equal to: *Our team equaled the other team's record.* –*n.* Person or thing that is equal: *In spelling she has no equal.*

• **error** /er' ər/ *n.* Mistake; something that is not the way it ought to be.

• **essay** /es' ā/ *n.* A short composition on a particular subject. /e sā'/ *v.* Try; attempt: *The student pilot essayed her first solo flight.*

f

• **factor** /fak' tər/ *n.* **1.** Any one of the causes that bring about a result: *Ability, industry, and health are factors in success at school.* **2.** Any of the numbers that produce a given number or quantity when multiplied together: *2 and 5 are factors of 10.*

• **faculty** /fak' əl tē/ *n.* **1.** Power to do something, especially power of the mind: *the faculty of hearing.* **2.** The teachers of a school, college, or university. *pl.* **faculties.**

• **fancy** /fan' sē/ *n.* **1.** Power to imagine. **2.**

/a/ ran /ā/ rain /ã/ care /ä/ car /e/ hen /ē/ he /ėr/ her /i/ in /ī/ ice /o/ not /ō/ no /ô/ off /u/ us /ū/ use /ü/ tool /ủ/ took /ou/ cow /oi/ boy /ch/ church /hw/ when /ng/ sing /sh/ ship /ᴛʜ/ this /th/ thin /zh/ vision /ə/ about, taken, pencil, lemon, circus

Liking. *pl.* **fancies.** —*v.* **1.** Imagine. **2.** Like; be fond of. **fancied, fancying.**

• **fatal** /fā′ təl/ *adj.* **1.** Causing death: *a fatal accident.* **2.** Causing great destruction; causing ruin: *The loss of all our money was fatal to our plans.* **3.** Important; fateful: *At last the fatal day of the contest arrived.*

• **faucet** /fô′ sət/ *n.* Device for turning on and off the flow of water; tap.

• **faulty** /fôl′ tē/ *adj.* Having faults; imperfect: *a faulty valve in the faucet.* **faultier, faultiest.**

• **favor** /fā′ vər/ *n.* **1.** Act of kindness: *do a favor.* **2.** Approval: *She looked with favor on our plan.* **3.** More than fair treatment: *Divide this candy without favor to anyone.* **4.** Small token given to a guest at a party. —*v.* **1.** Show kindness to; oblige: *He favored us with a song.* **2.** Like: *We favor this plan.* **3.** Give more than is fair to: *Our aunt favored my sister.* **4.** Help: *Darkness favored the enemy.* **5.** Look like.

• **fertile** /fėr′ təl/ *adj.* **1.** Able to bear seeds, fruit, or young: *a fertile plant or animal.* **2.** Fertilized: *Chickens hatch from fertile eggs.* **3.** Producing crops easily: *fertile soil.*

• **fervor** /fėr′ vər/ *n.* Great warmth of feeling; enthusiasm; earnestness: *The patriot's voice trembled with the fervor of her emotion.*

• **final** /fī′ nəl/ *adj.* **1.** At the end; coming last: *the final chapter of the book.* **2.** Settling the question: *The person in authority makes the final decision.*

• **firefly** /fīr′ flī′/ *n.* Small insect that gives off flashes of light when it flies at night. *pl.* **fireflies.**

• **fireproof** /fīr′ prüf′/ *v.* Make so that it will not burn, or not burn easily. —*adj.* That which will not burn, or not burn easily.

• **flannel** /flan′ əl/ *n.* A soft, warm, woolen or cotton cloth. —*adj.* Made of flannel.

• **flashlight** /flash′ līt′/ *n.* **1.** Light that flashes as a signal or warning. **2.** A portable electric light.

• **flavor** /flā′ vər/ *n.* Taste: *the flavor of chocolate.* —*v.* Give added taste to; season: *He flavored the sauce with vanilla.*

• **flexible** /flek′ sə bəl/ *adj.* Able to be bent without breaking; not stiff; easily bent in all directions: *Leather, rubber, and wire are flexible.*

• **floral** /flôr′ əl/ *adj.* Having to do with flowers: *floral designs.*

• **fluent** /flü′ ənt/ *adj.* **1.** Flowing smoothly or easily: *fluent speech.* **2.** Speaking or writing easily: *a fluent speaker.*

• **fluid** /flü′ id/ *n.* Any liquid or gas; something that will flow. —*v.* Like a liquid or gas; flowing: *She poured the fluid mass of candy into the dish to harden.*

• **folly** /fol′ ē/ *n.* **1.** Being foolish; lack of sense; unwise conduct: *It was folly to overeat at the picnic.* **2.** Foolish act, practice, or idea; something silly. *pl.* **follies.**

• **formal** /fôr′ məl/ *adj.* **1.** Not familiar and homelike: *A judge has a formal manner in the courtroom.* **2.** According to set rules or customs: *The ambassador made a formal call on the president.* **3.** Done with proper form: *A contract is a formal agreement.* —*n.* **1.** A formal dance or party. **2.** Formal dress; attire worn to a formal party.

• **forsake** /fôr sāk′/ *v.* Give up; leave; leave alone: *He ran away, forsaking his home and friends.* **forsook, forsaken, forsaking.**

• **forsook** /fôr su̇k′/ *See* **forsake.** *She forsook her family.*

• **fossil** /fos′ əl/ *n.* The hardened remains or trace of an animal or plant of a former age. —*adj.* **1.** Forming a fossil: *the fossil remains of a fern.* **2.** Belonging to the outworn past: *fossil ideas.*

• **foundry** /foun′ drē/ *n.* Place where metal is melted and molded; place where things are made of melted metal. *pl.* **foundries.**

• **fracture** /frak′ chər/ *n.* **1.** Breaking of a bone or cartilage. **2.** Being broken: *a fracture in the foundation of the building.* —*v.* Break; crack: *The girl fell and fractured her arm.* **fractured, fracturing.**

• **fragile** /fraj′ əl/ *adj.* Easily broken; delicate; frail: *a fragile glass; a fragile child.*

• **fragrant** /frā′ grənt/ *adj.* Sweet-smelling: *The rose is fragrant.*

• **freighter** /frāt′ ər/ *n.* Ship or aircraft that carries mainly freight.

• **frequent** /frē′ kwənt/ *adj.* Happening often, near together, or every little while: *frequent storms.*

• **friar** /frī′ ər/ *n.* Man who belongs to one of certain religious brotherhoods of the Roman Catholic church.

• **frugal** /frü′ gəl/ *adj.* **1.** Not wasteful; saving; using things well: *a frugal housekeeper.* **2.** Barely enough: *The poor woman ate a frugal supper of bread and milk.*

• **fuel** /fū′ əl/ *n.* **1.** Anything that can be burned

to make a useful fire. **2.** Anything that keeps up or increases a feeling: *The insults were fuel to his hatred.*

- **fully** /fu̇l′ ē/ *adv.* **1.** Completely. **2.** Abundantly. **3.** Quite.
- **funnel** /fun′ əl/ *n.* **1.** A tapering tube with a wide mouth shaped like a cone, used for pouring liquids, powders, or grains into a small opening without spilling. **2.** Smokestack or chimney on a steamship or steam engine.
- **furtive** /fėr′ tiv/ *adj.* **1.** Secret: *a furtive snatch at the candy.* **2.** Sly: *The thief had a furtive manner.*
- **futile** /fū′ təl/ *adj.* Useless; not successful: *futile efforts to put out the fire.*
- **future** /fū′ chər/ *n.* Time to come; what is to come. —*adj.* Coming; that will be.

g

- **galley** /gal′ ē/ *n.* **1.** A long, narrow ship of former times having oars and sails. **2.** Kitchen of a ship or airplane. *pl.* **galleys.**
- **gavel** /gav′ əl/ *n.* Small mallet used by a presiding officer to signal for order or attention: *The chairperson rapped on the table twice with his gavel.*
- **genius** /jē′ nē əs/ *n.* **1.** A very great natural power of mind. **2.** Person with such power. **3.** Great natural ability: *a genius for composing music.*
- **geyser** /gī′ zər/ *n.* Spring that sends up fountains or jets of hot water or steam.
- **gospel** /gos′ pəl/ *n.* **1.** Anything earnestly believed in. **2.** The absolute truth.
- **grammar** /gram′ ər/ *n.* **1.** Study of the forms and uses of words in sentences. **2.** Rules about the use of words. **3.** Use of words according to such rules: *The man's English grammar was full of mistakes.*
- **gravel** /grav′ əl/ *n.* Pebbles and pieces of rock coarser than sand, much used for roads and walks.
- **greedy** /grēd′ ē/ *adj.* **1.** Wanting to get more than one's share. **2.** Wanting to eat a great deal in a hurry. **greedier, greediest.**
- **grovel** /gruv′ əl/ *v.* Crawl at someone's feet; humble oneself: *The dog groveled before his master when he saw the whip.*
- **guideline** /gīd′ līn′/ *n.* **1.** A lightly marked line used as a guide for lettering or drawing. **2.** Rope or cord used to guide a person's steps. **3.** Any guide or indication of a future course of action: *The committee followed the guidelines set down by the club president.*
- **guilty** /gil′ tē/ *adj.* **1.** Having done wrong. **2.** Knowing or showing that one has done wrong: *You certainly have a guilty look.* **guiltier, guiltiest.**
- **gulley** /gul′ ē/ *n.* A narrow gorge; ditch made by heavy rains or running water. *pl.* **gullies.**

h

- **hamster** /ham′ stər/ *n.* Animal somewhat like a mouse, but larger, with a short tail and large cheek pouches.
- **handsome** /han′ səm/ *adj.* **1.** Good-looking. **2.** Fairly large; considerable: *She gave them a handsome sum of money.*
- **harbor** /här′ bər/ *n.* **1.** A place of shelter for ships. **2.** Any place of shelter: *The child fled to the harbor of his father's arms.* —*v.* **1.** Give shelter to: *The dog's shaggy fur harbors fleas.* **2.** Have and keep in mind: *She harbored plans for revenge on her enemies.*
- **harpoon** /här pün′/ *n.* Spear with a rope tied to it, used for catching whales and other sea animals. —*v.* Strike, catch, or kill with a harpoon.
- **harvest** /här′ vəst/ *n.* **1.** Reaping and gathering in of grain and other food crops. **2.** Time or season of the harvest. **3.** One season's yield of any natural product, crop. —*v.* Gather in and bring home for use.
- **hazel** /hā′ zəl/ *n.* Shrub or small tree whose light-brown nuts are good to eat. —*adj.* Light brown.
- **healthy** /hel′ thē/ *adj.* **1.** Having good health. **2.** Giving good health: *Exercise is healthy.* **healthier, healthiest.**
- **hearty** /här′ tē/ *n.* **1.** Warm and friendly; sincere: *a hearty welcome.* **2.** Strong and well; vigorous: *The old man was hale and hearty at eighty.* **3.** Nourishing: *a hearty meal.* **heartier, heartiest.**

• **heavy** /hev′ ē/ *adj.* **1.** Having much weight. **2.** Of more than usual weight for its kind. **3.** Greater than usual. **4.** Hard to bear or endure. **5.** Hard to deal with. **6.** Weighted down. **heavier, heaviest.**

• **heifer** /hef′ ər/ *n.* A young cow that has not had a calf.

• **helium** /hē′ lē əm/ *n.* A very light gas that will not burn, much used in balloons and dirigibles.

• **hermit** /hėr′ mit/ *n.* Person who goes away from other people and lives alone, often living a religious life.

• **hobby** /hob′ ē/ *n.* Something a person likes to work at or study which is not his or her main occupation. *pl.* **hobbies.**

• **hockey** /hok′ ē/ *n.* Game played by two teams on ice or on a field, with players hitting a rubber disk or ball with curved sticks to drive it across a goal.

• **holster** /hōl′ stər/ *n.* A leather case for a pistol, attached to a person's belt. A holster for a rifle is attached to a horseman's saddle.

• **honey** /hun′ ē/ *n.* **1.** A thick, sweet yellow liquid, good to eat, that bees make out of drops of nectar they collect from flowers. **2.** Sweetness. **3.** Darling; dear. *pl.* **honeys.**

• **honor** /on′ ər/ *n.* Glory; fame; good name. –*v.* Respect; think highly of.

• **horror** /hôr′ ər/ *n.* **1.** A shivering, shaking terror. **2.** Very strong dislike: *The child has a horror of spiders.* **3.** Thing that causes great fear.

• **household** /hous′ hōld′/ *n.* **1.** All people living in a house. **2.** A home and its affairs. –*adj.* Of a household.

• **housewife** /hous′ wīf′/ *n.* Woman who manages a home and its affairs. *pl.* **housewives.**

• **hovel** /huv′ əl/ *n.* House that is small, crude, and unpleasant to live in.

• **hover** /huv′ ər/ *v.* **1.** Stay in or near one place in the air: *The birds hovered over the field.* **2.** Wait near by: *The dogs hovered near the kitchen door at mealtime.* **3.** Be in an uncertain condition; waver: *The sick child hovered between life and death.*

• **humor** /hū′ mər/ *n.* **1.** Funny or amusing quality: *I see no humor in your tricks.* **2.** Ability to see or show the amusing or funny side of things: *Mark Twain was famous for his humor.* **3.** State of mind; mood: *in a good humor.* –*v.* Give in to a person's fancies or whims: *She tried to humor the sick child.*

• **hurry** /hėr′ ē/ *n.* A hurried movement or action. –*v.* Move, drive, carry, or send quickly. **hurried, hurries.**

• **hymnal** /him′ nəl/ *n.* A book of hymns.

i

• **ideal** /ī dē′ əl/ *n.* A perfect type; model to be imitated: *Her mother is her ideal.* –*adj.* Perfect; as one would wish: *an ideal day for a picnic.*

• **idiot** /id′ ē ət/ *n.* **1.** Person born with such a weak mind as never to be able to learn to read or to count; a very stupid person. **2.** A very foolish person.

• **ignite** /ig nīt′/ *v.* **1.** Set on fire: *ignite the match.* **2.** Begin to burn: *Gasoline ignites easily.* **ignited, igniting.**

• **image** /im′ ij/ *n.* **1.** Likeness: *image in a mirror.* **2.** Statue. **3.** Picture in the mind: *I can shut my eyes and see images of things and persons.*

• **impair** /im pãr′/ *v.* Make worse; damage; harm; weaken: *Poor food impaired his health.*

• **impeach** /im pēch′/ *v.* **1.** Accuse a public official of wrong conduct in office before a competent tribunal: *The judge was impeached for accepting a bribe.* **2.** Cast doubt on: *impeach a person's honor.*

• **impose** /im pōz′/ *v.* Put (a burden, tax, or punishment) on. **imposed, imposing.**

• **indeed** /in dēd′/ *adv.* In fact; in truth; really; surely.

• **inhale** /in hāl′/ *v.* Draw into the lungs; breathe in air, gas, fragrance, or tobacco smoke. **inhaled, inhaling.**

• **inquiry** /in′ kwər ē/ *n.* **1.** A question. **2.** A search for truth, information, or knowledge. **3.** Act of inquiring. *pl.* **inquiries.**

• **iodine** /ī′ ə dīn/ *n.* **1.** Substance used in medicine, in photography, and in making dyes. **2.** Brown liquid containing iodine, put on wounds to kill disease germs and prevent infection. [*Iodine* is derived from the Greek word *iodes,* meaning "violet-colored," the color of the vapor that rises from the substance.]

j

• **jackal** /jak′ əl/ *n.* A wild dog of Asia and Africa, about as big as a fox, said to eat what the lion leaves of its prey.

• **jersey** /jėr′ zē/ *n.* **1.** A close-fitting sweater that is pulled on over the head. **2.** A knitted cloth that is made by machine. *pl.* **jerseys.**

• **jewel** /jü′ əl/ *n.* **1.** Gem; precious stone. **2.** A valuable ornament to be worn, set with precious stones. **3.** Person or thing that is very precious. —*v.* Set or adorn with jewels or with things like jewels: *a sky jeweled with stars.*

• **jigsaw** /jig′ sô′/ *n.* A narrow saw mounted in a frame and worked with an up-and-down motion, used to cut curves.

• **jockey** /jok′ ē/ *n.* Person who rides horses in races as an occupation. *pl.* **jockeys.** —*v.* Maneuver so as to get advantage: *The crew jockeyed its boat into a good position.* **jockeyed, jockeying.**

• **journey** /jėr′ nē/ *n.* Traveling from one place to another; trip: *a journey around the world.* —*v.* Take a trip; travel: *journey to Europe. pl.* **journeys.** [*Journey* is derived from the old French word *journée,* meaning "a day's work or travel." It is taken from the Latin word *diurnus,* meaning "of a day."]

• **jovial** /jō′ vē əl/ *adj.* Good-humored and merry; full of fun. [*Jovial* is derived from the French word *jovial* and the Latin word *Jove,* name of the god Jupiter who was thought by the ancient Romans to be the source of happiness.]

• **jukebox** /jük′ boks′/ *n.* A machine that plays recordings after coins have been put in: *Is your favorite song on this jukebox?*

• **junkyard** /jungk′ yärd′/ *n.* Place where junk is sold.

• **juror** /jůr′ ər/ *n.* Member of a jury.

• **jury** /jůr′ ē/ *n.* **1.** Group of persons sworn to give a true answer to the question put before it in a court of law: *Is the accused person guilty or not?* **2.** Any group of persons chosen to give a judgment or decide a winner: *The jury of teachers gave her poem first prize. pl.* **juries.**

• **juvenile** /jü′ və nəl/ *adj.* **1.** Young; youthful: *a juvenile appearance.* **2.** Of or for boys and girls: *juvenile books.* —*n.* **1.** A young person: *A juvenile is not allowed to drive.* **2.** Book for boys and girls: *All the books in this section of the library are juveniles.*

k

• **kennel** /ken′ əl/ *n.* **1.** House for a dog. **2.** Place where dogs are bred.

• **kidney** /kid′ nē/ *n.* **1.** One of the pair of organs in the body that separate waste matter and water from the blood and pass them off through the bladder in liquid form. **2.** Kidney or kidneys of an animal, cooked for food. *pl.* **kidneys.**

• **kosher** /kō′ shər/ *adj.* Right or clean according to Jewish law: *kosher meat.*

l

• **label** /lā′ bəl/ *n.* Slip of paper or other material attached to something to show what or whose it is, or where it is to go. —*v.* **1.** Put or write a label on: *The bottle is labeled "Poison."* **2.** Call; name; put in a class: *He labeled the boastful boy a liar.*

• **labor** /lā′ bər/ *n.* **1.** Work; toil. **2.** Workers as a group. —*v.* **1.** Do work; toil. **2.** Move slowly and heavily: *The old car labored up the hill.*

• **language** /lang′ gwij/ *n.* **1.** Human speech, spoken or written. **2.** The speech of one nation. **3.** Form, style, or kind of language. **4.** Wording; words. **5.** The expression of thoughts and feelings otherwise than by words.

• **lawsuit** /lô′ süt′/ *n.* Case in a court of law started by one person to claim something from another; application to a court for justice.

• **lecture** /lek′ chər/ *n.* **1.** Speech; planned talk on a certain subject. **2.** Scolding. —*v.* **1.** Give a lecture. **2.** Scold. **lectured, lecturing.**

• **legal** /lē′ gəl/ *n.* **1.** Of the law: *legal knowledge.* **2.** According to law; lawful: *Hunting is legal only during certain seasons.*

• **legible** /lej′ ə bəl/ *adj.* **1.** Able to be read. **2.** Easy to read; plain and clear: *a legible handwriting.*

• **leisure** /lē′ zhər/ *n.* Free time from required work in which persons may rest, amuse themselves, and do the things they like to do. —*adj.* Free, not busy: *leisure hours.*

• **lentil** /len′ təl/ *n.* Vegetable much like a bean, cooked like peas and often eaten in soup.

/a/ ran /ā/ rain /ã/ care /ä/ car /e/ hen /ē/ he /ėr/ her /i/ in /ī/ ice /o/ not /ō/ no /ô/ off /u/ us /ū/ use /ü/ tool /ů/ took /ou/ cow /oi/ boy /ch/ church /hw/ when /ng/ sing /sh/ ship /ᴛʜ/ this /th/ thin /zh/ vision /ə/ about, taken, pencil, lemon, circus

• **level** /lev′ əl/ *adj.* **1.** Flat; even: *a level field.* **2.** Of equal height or importance: *The table is level with the window sill.* —*v.* **1.** Make level: *The builder leveled the ground with a bulldozer.* **2.** Aim: *level a gun at the target.* —*n.* **1.** Instrument for showing whether a surface is level. **2.** Height: *the level of the water.*

• **likable** /lī′ kə bəl/ *adj.* Pleasing; popular; having qualities that win good will or friendship.

• **likewise** /līk′ wīs′/ *adv.* **1.** The same. **2.** Also; moreover; too.

• **liquor** /lik′ ər/ *n.* **1.** Drink, such as brandy or whiskey. **2.** Any liquid: *Pickles are put up in a salty liquor.*

• **livestock** /līv′ stok′/ *n.* Farm animals such as cows, horses, sheep, and pigs.

• **local** /lō′ kəl/ *adj.* **1.** Having something to do with a certain place or places: *the local doctor.* **2.** Of just one part of the body: *a local pain.* **3.** Making all, or almost all, stops: *a local train.*

• **loyal** /loi′ əl/ *adj.* **1.** True and faithful to love, a promise, or duty: *a loyal worker.* **2.** Faithful to one's country, government, or leader: *a loyal citizen.*

• **lunar** /lü′ nər/ *adj.* **1.** Having to do with the moon: *a lunar eclipse.* **2.** Like the moon.

m

• **magic** /maj′ ik/ *n.* **1.** The pretended art of making things happen by secret charms. **2.** Something that produces results as if by magic. —*adj.* Done by magic.

• **mailbox** /māl′ boks′/ *n.* **1.** A public box from which mail is collected. **2.** A private box to which mail is delivered. *pl.* **mailboxes.**

• **maintain** /mān tān′/ *v.* **1.** Keep; keep up: *One must maintain a footing in a tug of war.* **2.** Support: *maintain an opinion.* **3.** Keep in good repair: *maintain a fleet of cars.* **4.** Declare to be true: *He maintained that he was innocent.*

• **major** /mā′ jər/ *adj.* Larger, greater: *the major part of his life.* —*n.* An army, air force, or marine officer ranking next above a captain.

• **mammal** /mam′ əl/ *n.* Any of a class of animals that are warm-blooded, that have a backbone, and that feed their young with milk from the mother's breasts.

• **manager** /man′ ə jər/ *n.* Person who manages.

• **mankind** /man′ kīnd′/ *n.* The human race; all human beings. /man′ kīnd′/ *n.* Men: *Mankind and womankind both like praise.*

• **marshal** /mär′ shəl/ *n.* **1.** Officer; police officer with duties like those of a sheriff. **2.** Person in charge of events or ceremonies. —*v.* **1.** Arrange in proper order: *She carefully marshaled her facts for the debate.* **2.** Conduct with ceremony: *The ambassador was marshaled into the presence of the king.*

• **marvel** /mär′ vəl/ *n.* Something wonderful; astonishing thing: *The airplane is a marvel of science.* —*v.* Be filled with astonishment: *I marveled at the beautiful sunset.*

• **massage** /mə säzh′/ *n.* Rubbing and kneading of the muscles and joints to make them work better and to increase circulation of the blood. —*v.* Give a massage to. **massaged, massaging.**

• **massive** /mas′ iv/ *adj.* **1.** Big and heavy; large and solid: *a massive wrestler.* **2.** Giving the impression of being large and solid: *a massive forehead.*

• **matron** /mā′ trən/ *n.* **1.** Wife or widow, especially an older married woman. **2.** Woman who manages the household affairs of an institution or has charge of the women in a jail.

• **mattress** /mat′ rəs/ *n.* Covering of strong cloth stuffed with cotton, straw, etc., used on a bed or as a bed. A spring mattress contains wire springs.

• **meanwhile** /mēn′ hwīl′/ *n., adv.* Meantime.

• **mediate** /mē′ dē āt/ *v.* Come in to help settle a dispute: *Mother mediated in the quarrel between my brothers.* **mediated, mediating.**

• **medium** /mē′ dē əm/ *adj.* **1.** Having a middle position, quality, or condition. **2.** In the middle; neither one extreme or the other: *a happy medium between city and country life.* **3.** Substance or agent through which something acts: *Copper wire is a medium of electrical transmission.* **4.** Environment: *Fish live in the medium of water. pl.* **mediums** or **media** /mē′ dē ə/.

• **medley** /med′ lē/ *n.* **1.** A mixture of things that do not ordinarily belong together. **2.** Piece of music made up of parts from other pieces. *pl.* **medleys.**

• **melody** /mel′ ə dē/ *n.* **1.** Sweet music. **2.** A tune. **3.** The main tune in harmony. *pl.* **melodies.**

• **menace** /men′ əs/ *n.* Threat: *Forest fires are a great menace in dry weather.* —*v.* Threaten:

Floods menaced the towns in the valley. **menaced, menacing.**

- **mental** /men′ təl/ *adj.* **1.** Of the mind: *a mental test.* **2.** For the mind; done by the mind: *mental arithmetic.* **3.** For people having a disease of the mind: *a mental hospital.*
- **merchant** /mėr′ chənt/ *n.* **1.** Person who buys and sells. **2.** Storekeeper. *—adj.* Trading; having something to do with trade: *merchant ships.*
- **message** /mes′ ij/ *n.* **1.** Words sent from one person to another. **2.** An official speech or writing. **3.** Lesson or moral contained in a story, play, or speech.
- **meteor** /mē′ tē ər/ *n.* Mass of stone or metal that comes toward the earth from outer space with enormous speed; shooting star.
- **migrate** /mī′ grāt/ *v.* **1.** Move from one place to settle in another. **2.** Go from one region to another with the change in seasons: *Birds sometimes migrate to warmer countries in the winter.* **migrated, migrating.**
- **minor** /mī′ nər/ *adj.* Smaller; lesser; less important: *a minor error.* *—n.* A person under the legal age of responsibility.
- **mirage** /mə räzh′/ *n.* An illusion, usually in the desert, at sea, or on a paved road, in which a distant scene appears to be closer than it actually is.
- **mirror** /mir′ ər/ *n.* Glass in which you can see yourself; looking glass. *—v.* Reflect as a mirror does: *The water mirrored the trees along the bank.*
- **mobile** /mō′ bəl/ *adj.* **1.** Movable; easy to move: *Arms and legs are mobile.* **2.** Moving easily; changing easily: *A mobile mind is one that is easily moved by ideas or feelings.*
- **model** /mod′ əl/ *n.* **1.** Small copy. **2.** Style. **3.** Thing or person to be copied or imitated. **4.** Person who poses for artists or photographers. **5.** Person who puts on garments to show customers how they look. *—v.* **1.** Make; shape; fashion; design. **2.** Follow as a model. *—adj.* Just right or perfect, especially in conduct: *a model child.*
- **molar** /mō′ lər/ *n.* Tooth with a broad surface for grinding: *A person's back teeth are molars.*
- **money** /mun′ ē/ *n.* **1.** Coins or paper notes issued by a government, for use in buying and selling. **2.** Wealth. *pl.* **moneys.**
- **mongrel** /mong′ grəl/ *n.* Animal or plant of mixed breed, especially a dog. *—adj.* Of mixed breed, race, origin, or nature.
- **monitor** /mon′ ə tər/ *n.* **1.** Pupil in school with special duties. **2.** Person or device that gives warning; person who gives advice.
- **monkey** /mung′ kē/ *n.* **1.** An animal of the group most like humans. **2.** Person, especially a child, who is full of mischief. *pl.* **monkeys.**
- **moonlight** /mün′ līt′/ *n.* Light of the moon. *—adj.* Having the light of the moon.
- **moral** /môr′ əl/ *adj.* **1.** Right; just; good in conduct: *a moral act.* **2.** Capable of understanding right and wrong: *A baby is not a moral being.* **3.** Teaching a good lesson: *a moral story.* *—n.* Lesson; inner meaning or teaching of a story, fable, or event: *The moral of the story was "Look before you leap."*
- **morsel** /môr′ səl/ *n.* Small bite; a piece; fragment; mouthful.
- **mortal** /môr′ təl/ *adj.* **1.** Sure to die at some time: *a mortal creature.* **2.** Having to do with human beings: *mortal flesh.* **3.** Causing death: *a mortal wound.* **4.** Very great: *mortal terror.* **5.** Causing death of a soul: *mortal sin.* *—n.* **1.** Human being: *No mortal could have survived the fire.* **2.** Being that is sure to die: *All creatures are mortals.*
- **mortar** /môr′ tər/ *n.* **1.** Mixture of lime, cement, sand, and water for holding bricks or stones together. **2.** Very short cannon for shooting shells or fireworks high into the air. **3.** Bowl of porcelain, glass, or other hard material, in which substances may be pounded to a powder.
- **motive** /mō′ tiv/ *n.* Thought or feeling that makes one act. *—adj.* Causing movement: *the motive power of steam or electricity.*
- **mural** /mūr′ əl/ *adj.* On a wall: *In that mansion there are many mural paintings.* *—n.* A picture painted on a wall.
- **muscle** /mus′ əl/ *n.* **1.** The tissue in the bodies of people and animals that can be tightened or loosened to make the body move. **2.** Strength.

• **myself** /mī′ self′/ *pron.* The same as I. *pl.* **ourselves.**

n

• **nasal** /nā′ zəl/ *adj.* **1.** Of, in, or from the nose. **2.** Spoken through the nose: *nasal sounds.* —*n.* A nasal sound: *Some sounds in English are nasals.*

• **native** /nā′ tiv/ *n.* **1.** A person born in a certain place or country. **2.** One of the original inhabitants of a place, as contrasted with settlers, visitors, etc. —*adj.* **1.** Born in a certain place or country. **2.** Belonging to a person because of birth, country, or race. **3.** Born in a person: *native talent.* **4.** Having to do with the original inhabitants.

• **nature** /nā′ chər/ *n.* **1.** The world; all things except those made by humans. **2.** The regular way in which things are and act. **3.** What a thing really is; quality; character.

• **nearly** /nir′ lē/ *adv.* **1.** Almost: *It is nearly midnight.* **2.** Closely.

• **necktie** /nek′ tī′/ *n.* A tie worn around the neck, under the collar of a shirt, and tied in front.

• **nectar** /nek′ tər/ *n.* **1.** The drink of the gods in ancient Greek myths. **2.** A sweet liquid found in many flowers, gathered by bees and made into honey.

• **neon** /nē′ on/ *n.* A colorless, odorless gas which is a chemical element forming a very small part of the air. Tubes containing neon are used in electric signs or lamps giving off a fiery red glow.

• **network** /net′ wėrk′/ *n.* **1.** Any system of lines that cross: *a network of railroads; a network of vines.* **2.** Group of radio or television stations that work together, so that what is broadcast by one may be broadcast by all.

• **nickel** /nik′ əl/ *n.* **1.** Metal that looks like silver and is somewhat like iron, much used in mixtures with other metals. **2.** A United States or Canadian five-cent piece containing a mixture of copper and nickel. [*Nickel* is shortened from *kupfernickel,* meaning "copper devil," because even though the metal ore looked like copper, it yielded none.]

• **nightgown** /nīt′ goun′/ *n.* A long, loose garment worn in bed.

• **nomad** /nō′ mad/ *n.* **1.** Member of a tribe that moves from place to place for better pasture. **2.** Wanderer.

• **normal** /nôr′ məl/ *adj.* **1.** Regular; usual: *The normal temperature of the human body is 98.6 degrees.* **2.** Not diseased, insane, or defective. —*n.* The usual state or condition: *He is ten pounds above normal for his age.*

• **nostril** /nos′ trəl/ *n.* Either of the two openings in the nose through which air is breathed into the lungs and smells come into the sensitive parts of the nose.

• **notebook** /nōt′ bůk′/ *n.* Book in which to write notes of things to be learned or remembered.

• **novel** /nov′ əl/ *adj.* Strange; new: *Flying gives people a novel sensation.* —*n.* Story with characters and a plot, long enough to fill one or more volumes.

• **nucleus** /nü′ klē əs/ *or* /nū′ klē əs/ *n.* **1.** Central part or thing around which other parts or things are collected. **2.** A beginning to which additions are made: *A five-dollar bill became the nucleus of a flourishing bank account.* **3.** The central part of an atom. *pl.* **nuclei** /nü′ klē ī/ *or* /nū′ klē ī/, **nucleuses.**

o

• **oasis** /ō ā′ sis/ *n.* Fertile spot in the desert where there is water. *pl.* **oases.**

• **odor** /ō′ dər/ *n.* Smell: *the odor of roses; the odor of garbage.*

• **offense** /ə fens′/ *n.* **1.** Breaking the law; sin: *The punishment for the offense is two years in prison.* **2.** Hurt feelings: *cause offense.* **3.** Hurting someone's feelings: *I meant no offense.* **4.** Something that offends or causes displeasure. **5.** Act of attacking: *offense against the enemy.*

• **office** /ôf′ is/ *n.* **1.** Room or rooms in which to work. **2.** Position, especially a public position. **3.** Duty of one's position. **4.** Staff of persons carrying on work in an office. **5.** Attention.

• **oilcloth** /oil′ klôth′/ *n.* **1.** Cloth made waterproof by coating it with paint. **2.** Cloth made waterproof by treating it with oil. *pl.* **oilcloths.**

• **only** /ōn′ lē/ *adj.* **1.** By itself; one and no more. **2.** Best; finest. —*adv.* **1.** Just; merely. **2.** And nothing more.

• **onward** /ôn′ wərd/ *adv., adj.* On; further on; toward the front; forward.

• **opal** /ō′ pəl/ *n.* Gem that shows beautiful changes of color, commonly milky white with colors.

• **opium** /ō′ pē əm/ *n.* An addicting and dangerous drug that causes sleep and eases pain, made from a kind of poppy.

• **oral** /ôr′ əl/ *adj.* **1.** Spoken: *An oral agreement is not enough.* **2.** Having to do with the mouth: *The oral opening in an earthworm is small.*

• **orbit** /ôr′ bit/ *n.* **1.** Path of the earth or any one of the planets about the sun. **2.** Path of any heavenly body around another heavenly body. **3.** Path of a scientifically constructed satellite around the earth. *–v.* Travel around the earth or some other heavenly body in an orbit.

• **orient** /ôr′ ē ənt/ *n.* **1.** The east. **2. The Orient,** the East; eastern countries. /ôr′ ē ent/ *v.* Place in the right position; place in any indicated direction: *The building is oriented north and south.*

• **oriole** /ôr′ ē ōl/ *n.* **1.** Any of several American birds having yellow and black or orange and black feathers. **2.** Any of several European birds having yellow and black feathers.

• **outlaw** /out′ lô′/ *n.* **1.** A lawless person; criminal. **2.** Person outside the protection of the law. *–v.* **1.** Make or declare unlawful. **2.** Make or declare an outlaw.

• **outweigh** /out′ wā′/ *v.* **1.** Weigh more than. **2.** Exceed in value, importance, or influence.

• **oval** /ō′ vəl/ *adj.* Shaped like an egg; shaped like an ellipse. *–n.* Something having an oval shape.

p

• **panel** /pan′ əl/ *n.* **1.** Strip or surface that is different in some way from what is around it. **2.** Members of a jury. **3.** Board containing instruments used in operating an automobile, aircraft, or other mechanism. **4.** Discussion group. *–v.* Arrange in panels; furnish or decorate with panels: *The dining room walls are paneled with oak.*

• **panic** /pan′ ik/ *n.* Unreasoning fear: *a spreading panic.* *–v.* Be affected with panic: *The audience panicked when the theater caught fire.* **panicked, panicking.** [*Panic* comes from the name of the Greek god *Pan,* whose appearance was thought to cause terror among people who saw him.]

• **parcel** /pär′ səl/ *n.* **1.** Bundle of things wrapped together; package. **2.** Piece: *a parcel of land.* **3.** Lot; pack: *The peddler had a whole parcel of odds and ends in his sack.*

• **parley** /pär′ lē/ *n.* Conference to discuss terms or matters in a dispute. *–v.* Discuss matters, especially with an enemy. *pl.* **parleys.**

• **parsley** /pär′ slē/ *n.* A garden plant with finely divided, fragrant leaves, used to flavor food and to trim platters of meat or fish. *pl.* **parsleys.**

• **party** /pär′ tē/ *n.* **1.** Group of people having a good time together. **2.** Group of people doing something together: *a scouting party.* **3.** Group of people organized to gain political influence: *Democratic Party.* **4.** Person: *The party you are telephoning is out.* *pl.* **parties.**

• **pastor** /pas′ tər/ *n.* Minister in charge of a church; spiritual guide.

• **pasture** /pas′ chər/ *n.* **1.** Grassy land on which cattle, sheep, and horses can feed. **2.** Grass and other growing plants: *These lands afford good pasture.* *–v.* **1.** Put animals out to pasture. **2.** Feed on growing grass. **pastured, pasturing.**

• **patent** /pat′ ənt/ *n.* A government grant giving a person rights over a new invention for a number of years. *–v.* Get such rights. *–adj.* Open, plain: *It is patent that he is guilty.*

• **patio** /pat′ ē ō/ *n.* **1.** An inner court or yard open to the sky. **2.** Terrace for outdoor eating or lounging. *pl.* **patios.**

• **payroll** /pā′ rōl′/ *n.* **1.** List of persons to be paid and the amount that each one is to receive. **2.** The total amount to be paid to them.

• **penalty** /pen′ əl tē/ *n.* **1.** Punishment: *The penalty for speeding is a fine of $10.* **2.** Disadvantage placed on a side or player for breaking the rules of some game or contest. *pl.* **penalties.**

• **peril** /per′ əl/ *n.* Chance of harm; danger: *Cross this dangerous road at your peril.* *–v.* Put in danger.

• **perspire** /pər spīr′/ *v.* Sweat: *The farmer perspired in the hot sun.* **perspired, perspiring.**

/a/ ran /ā/ rain /ã/ care /ä/ car /e/ hen /ē/ he /ėr/ her /i/ in /ī/ ice /o/ not /ō/ no /ô/ off /u/ us /ū/ use /ü/ tool /ů/ took /ou/ cow /oi/ boy /ch/ church /hw/ when /ng/ sing /sh/ ship /ᴛʜ/ this /th/ thin /zh/ vision /ə/ about, taken, pencil, lemon, circus

• **petal** /pet′ əl/ *n.* One of the leaflike parts of the blossom of a flowering plant: *A rose has many petals.*

• **piecemeal** /pēs′ mēl′/ *adv.* **1.** Piece by piece; a little at a time: *work done piecemeal.* **2.** To pieces; into fragments; into bits: *The lamb was torn piecemeal by the wolves.*

• **piety** /pī′ ə tē/ *n.* **1.** Reverence for a deity; holiness, goodness. **2.** A pious act, remark, or belief. *pl.* **pieties.**

• **pillar** /pil′ ər/ *n.* **1.** Column; slender, upright support usually made of stone, wood, or metal. **2.** An important support or supporter: *That woman is a pillar of the church.*

• **pinpoint** /pin′ point′/ *n.* **1.** The point of a pin. **2.** A trifle. *—v.* Describe or locate exactly: *The engineer pinpointed the trouble in the motor.* *—adj.* Exact: *pinpoint workmanship.*

• **pity** /pit′ ē/ *n.* **1.** Sympathy. **2.** Cause for pity or regret; thing to be sorry for. *pl.* **pities.** *—v.* Feel pity for. **pitied, pitying.**

• **pleasure** /plezh′ ər/ *n.* **1.** Feeling of being pleased. **2.** Something that pleases.

• **plural** /plu̇r′ əl/ *adj.* **1.** More than one in number: *"Boy" is singular; "boys" is plural.* **2.** Showing more than one in number: *a plural noun.* *—n.* Form of a noun that shows it means more than one: *"Books" is the plural of "book."*

• **plywood** /plī′ wu̇d′/ *n.* Board or boards made of thin layers of wood glued together.

• **podium** /pō′ dē əm/ *n.* A raised platform. *pl.* **podiums, podia** /pō′ dē ə/.

• **polar** /pō′ lər/ *adj.* Having to do with the North or South Pole; near the North or South Pole: *the polar regions; polar bear.*

• **policy**[1] /pol′ ə sē/ *n.* Plan of action; way of management: *government policies; It is a poor policy to promise more than you can do.* *pl.* **policies.**

• **policy**[2] /pol′ ə sē/ *n.* A written agreement about insurance. *pl.* **policies.**

• **pommel** /pom′ əl/ *or* /pum′ əl/ *n.* **1.** Part of the saddle that sticks up in front. **2.** A rounded knob on the hilt of a sword. *—v.* Strike or beat with the fists; pummel.

• **poplar** /pop′ lər/ *n.* **1.** Tree, like the cottonwood, that grows rapidly and produces light, soft wood. **2.** Wood of the poplar tree.

• **portal** /pôr′ təl/ *n.* Door; gate; entrance, usually an impressive one.

• **possible** /pos′ ə bəl/ *adj.* **1.** Can be done; can be. **2.** Can be true as a fact.

• **postal** /pōst′ əl/ *adj.* Having to do with mail and post offices: *a postal clerk; postal regulations.*

• **poster** /pōst′ ər/ *n.* A large printed sheet or notice put up in some public place.

• **poultry** /pōl′ trē/ *n.* Birds raised for their meat or eggs, such as chickens, turkeys, geese, or ducks.

• **practical** /prak′ tik əl/ *adj.* **1.** Useful. **2.** Having to do with action or practice rather than thought or theory. **3.** Fit for actual practice: *a practical plan.* **4.** Having good sense: *a practical person.* **practical joke,** a trick played on someone.

• **pretzel** /pretz′ əl/ *n.* A hard biscuit in the form of a knot, salted on the outside.

• **problem** /prob′ ləm/ *n.* **1.** Question; difficult question. **2.** Matter of doubt or difficulty. *—adj.* That causes difficulty.

• **pulley** /pu̇l′ ē/ *n.* Wheel with a hollowed rim in which a rope can run and so lift weights, or change the direction of a pull: *Raise the flag to the top of the pole by a rope and two pulleys.*

• **pummel** /pum′ əl/ *v.* Strike or beat; beat with the fists; pommel.

• **punctual** /pungk′ chü əl/ *adj.* On time; prompt: *a punctual worker.*

• **pupil**[1] /pū′ pəl/ *n.* Person who is learning in school or is being taught by someone.

• **pupil**[2] /pū′ pəl/ *n.* The black center of the eye where light enters.

• **purchase** /pėr′ chəs/ *v.* **1.** Buy; get by paying a price. **2.** Get in return for something: *purchase safety at the cost of happiness.* **purchased, purchasing.** *—n.* **1.** Act of buying. **2.** Thing bought: *Her hat was a good purchase.*

• **pursue** /pər sü′/ *v.* **1.** Follow in order to catch or kill; chase. **2.** Strive for; try to get: *pursue pleasure.* **3.** Keep on with: *pursue the study of art.* **pursued, pursuing.**

q

• **qualify** /kwol′ ə fī/ *v.* **1.** Make fit or competent: *Can you qualify for the job?* **2.** Become fit; show oneself fit. **3.** Limit; change somewhat; make less strong: *qualify a statement.* **qualified, qualifying.**

• **query** /kwir′ ē/ *n.* Question. *pl.* **queries.** *—v.* **1.** Ask about; inquire into. **2.** Express doubt about. **queried, querying.**

• **quicksand** /kwik′ sand′/ *n.* Soft wet sand, very deep, that will not hold up one's weight.

Quicksand may swallow up people and animals.

- **quinine** /kwī' nīn/ *n.* A bitter medicine used for malaria and fevers.

r

- **radiate** /rā' dē āt/ *v.* **1.** Give out rays of: *radiate heat and light.* **2.** Send forth: *Her face radiated joy.* **3.** Spread out from a center: *Roads radiate from the city in all directions.* **radiated, radiating.**
- **radium** /rā' dē əm/ *n.* A rare metal that gives off powerful rays, much used in the treatment of cancer.
- **radius** /rā' dē əs/ *n.* **1.** Any line going straight from the center to the outside of a circle or sphere: *A spoke of a wheel is a radius.* **2.** A circular area measured by the length of its radius: *The explosion could be heard within a radius of ten miles. pl.* **radiuses** or **radii** /rā' dē ī/.
- **rally** /ral' ē/ *v.* **1.** Bring together again: *rally the fleeing troops.* **2.** Come together for a common purpose; come together to help: *rally to help the injured.* **3.** Recover strength or health: *The sick man rallied and spoke to his family.* **rallied, rallying.** *—n.* Meeting of many people. *pl.* **rallies.**
- **ransom** /ran' səm/ *n.* Price paid or demanded before a captive is set free: *The robbers held the travelers prisoners for ransom.* *—v.* **1.** Obtain the release of a captive by paying a price: *They ransomed the kidnaped child with a great sum of money.* **2.** Redeem.
- **rascal** /ras' kəl/ *n.* **1.** A bad, dishonest person. **2.** A mischievous person: *Come here, you little rascal.*
- **ravel** /rav' əl/ *v.* **1.** Fray out; spread into threads: *My sweater has raveled at the elbow.* **2.** Tangle; involve; confuse. **raveled, raveling.**
- **ready** /red' ē/ *adj.* **1.** Prepared for action or use at once. **2.** Willing. **3.** Prompt. **4.** Likely; likable. **5.** Easy to reach. **readier, readiest.** *—v.* Make ready. **readied, readying.**
- **rebel** /reb' əl/ *n.* Person who resists or fights against authority instead of obeying. *—adj.* Defying authority or law: *a rebel army.* /rē bel'/ *v.* **1.** Feel a great dislike or opposition: *We rebelled at having to miss the picnic.* **2.** Resist or fight against authority: *The harassed soldiers decided to rebel.* **rebelled, rebelling.**
- **regular** /reg' ū lər/ *adj.* **1.** Fixed by custom or rule. **2.** According to rule. **3.** Steady; habitual. **4.** Well-balanced; even in size, spacing, or speed.
- **remedy** /rem' ə dē/ *n.* A cure. *pl.* **remedies.** *—v.* Cure; put right; make right. **remedied, remedying.**
- **rental** /ren' təl/ *n.* Amount received or paid as rent: *The yearly rental of her house is $2500.*
- **reptile** /rep' təl/ *n.* A cold-blooded animal such as the snake, crocodile, alligator, lizard, or turtle, that creeps or crawls.
- **rescue** /res' kū/ *n.* Saving or freeing from harm or danger. *—v.* Save from danger, capture, or harm. **rescued, rescuing.**
- **revel** /rev' əl/ *n.* Merrymaking; a noisy good time. *—v.* **1.** Take pleasure: *The children revel in country life.* **2.** Make merry.
- **rival** /rī' vəl/ *n.* Person who tries to equal or do better than another: *rivals in sports; rivals for the same class office.* *—v.* **1.** Try to equal or outdo. **2.** Equal or match: *The sunset rivaled the sunrise in beauty.* *—adj.* Wanting the same thing as another: *rival stores; rival players; rival teams.*
- **rodeo** /rō dā' ō/ *or* /rō' dē ō/ *n.* **1.** Contest in roping cattle, riding horses, etc. **2.** The driving of cattle together. *pl.* **rodeos.**
- **rotor** /rō' tər/ *n.* **1.** The rotating part of a machine or apparatus. **2.** System of rotating blades by which a helicopter is able to fly.
- **roughneck** /ruf' nek'/ *n.* A rough, coarse, or violent person.
- **royal** /roi' əl/ *adj.* **1.** Having to do with kings or queens: *the royal family of England.* **2.** Of a kingdom: *the royal army.* **3.** Appropriate for a king; splendid: *a royal feast.* **4.** Noble; majestic: *The lion is a royal beast.*
- **rummage** /rum' ij/ *v.* Search in a disorderly way: *I rummaged in my drawer for a pair of gloves.* **rummaged, rummaging.** *—n.* A thorough search.
- **rumor** /rü' mər/ *n.* **1.** Story or statement talked of as news without any proof that it

---

/a/ ran /ā/ rain /ã/ care /ä/ car /e/ hen /ē/ he /ėr/ her /i/ in /ī/ ice /o/ not /ō/ no /ô/ off /u/ us /ū/ use /ü/ tool /u̇/ took /ou/ cow /oi/ boy /ch/ church /hw/ when /ng/ sing /sh/ ship /ᴛʜ/ this /th/ thin /zh/ vision /ə/ about, taken, pencil, lemon, circus

is true. **2.** Vague, general talk: *Rumor has it that the new girl went to school in France.* —*v.* Tell or spread by rumor: *It is rumored that taxes will be increased next year.*

• **rural** /rür′ əl/ *adj.* In the country; belonging to the country; like that of the country: *Rural life is usually quiet.*

S

• **salute** /sə lüt′/ *v.* **1.** Honor in a formal manner by raising the hand to the head, by firing guns, or by dipping flags. **2.** Greet. **saluted, saluting.** —*n.* Act of saluting; sign of welcome or honor: *She bowed in response to the salutes of the crowd.*

• **sandal** /san′ dəl/ *n.* **1.** Kind of shoe made of a sole fastened to the foot by straps. **2.** Kind of slipper.

• **sandbag** /sand′ bag′/ *n.* A bag filled with sand. —*v.* **1.** Place sandbags by for reinforcement. **2.** Hit with, or as if with, a sandbag.

• **satchel** /sach′ əl/ *n.* A small bag, especially one for carrying clothes or books.

• **satin** /sat′ ən/ *n.* Silk or rayon cloth with one very smooth glossy side. —*adj.* Like satin; smooth and glossy.

• **savage** /sav′ ij/ *n.* Fierce, brutal or cruel person. —*adj.* **1.** Not civilized: *savage customs.* **2.** Fierce, cruel, ready to fight. **3.** Wild, rugged: *She liked the savage mountain scenery.*

• **savor** /sā′ vər/ *n.* Taste or smell; flavor: *The soup has the savor of onion.* —*v.* **1.** Enjoy the flavor of: *He savors roast beef.* **2.** Season: *Onion savors soup.* **3.** Have the quality or nature of: *The plot savored of treason.*

• **scandal** /skan′ dəl/ *n.* **1.** A shameful action that brings disgrace or shocks public opinion. **2.** Disgrace; damage to reputation. **3.** Evil gossip; slander.

• **scholar** /skol′ ər/ *n.* **1.** A learned person: *The professor was a famous Latin scholar.* **2.** Pupil at school; learner.

• **scissors** /siz′ ərz/ *n.* Tool or instrument for cutting that has two sharp blades fastened so that they will work toward each other. *pl.* or *sing.*

• **scoundrel** /skoun′ drəl/ *n.* A bad person without honor or good principles; villain; rascal.

• **sculptor** /skulp′ tər/ *n.* Person who carves or models figures of bronze or marble or other substances.

• **scurry** /skėr′ ē/ *v.* Run quickly; scamper; hurry: *The mice scurried into the hole in the wall.* **scurried, scurrying.** —*n.* Hurrying: *With much scurry and fuss, he got started at last.* *pl.* **scurries.**

• **sector** /sek′ tər/ *n.* **1.** A designated area within a military zone for which a military unit is responsible. **2.** A section of a circle.

• **sentinel** /sen′ tə nəl/ *n.* Person stationed to keep watch and guard against surprises.

• **sequel** /sē′ kwəl/ *n.* Something that follows as a result of an earlier happening; outcome.

• **serial** /sir′ ē əl/ *n.* Story published one part at a time. —*adj.* Of a series.

• **serpent** /sėr′ pənt/ *n.* Snake, especially a big snake.

• **service** /sėr′ vis/ *n.* **1.** Helpful act or acts; aid. **2.** Supply; arrangements for supplying: *The train service was good.* **3.** Occupation or employment as a servant. **4.** Work for others: *the service of a doctor.* **5.** Advantage; benefit. **6.** Department of government or public employment: *The service often means the army, navy, or air force.* **7.** Religious ceremony. **8.** Manner of serving food: *the service in a restaurant.* —*v.* Make fit for service: *The mechanic serviced our car.* **serviced, servicing.**

• **shampoo** /sham pü′/ *v.* Wash the hair. **shampooed, shampooing.** —*n.* **1.** Washing the hair. **2.** Preparation used for shampooing. *pl.* **shampoos.**

• **shotgun** /shot′ gun′/ *n.* Gun with no grooves in its barrel, for firing cartridges filled with small shot.

• **shovel** /shuv′ əl/ *n.* Tool with a broad scoop, used to lift and throw loose matter. —*v.* **1.** Lift and throw with a shovel. **2.** Make with a shovel: *shovel a path.* **3.** Lift and throw as with a shovel: *The hungry man shoveled food into his mouth.*

• **shrivel** /shriv′ əl/ *v.* Dry up; wither; shrink and wrinkle: *The hot sunshine shriveled the grass.*

• **signal** /sig′ nəl/ *n.* Notice of something. —*v.* **1.** Make a signal or signals to: *He signaled to the car to stop.* **2.** Make known by a signal or signals: *The bell signaled the end of the class period.* —*adj.* **1.** Used as a signal: *a signal flag.* **2.** Remarkable; striking: *The airplane was a signal invention.*

• **singular** /sing′ gū lər/ *adj.* **1.** Exceptional; superior. **2.** Queer; strange: *They were puzzled by the singular behavior of the boys.*

3. One in number: *"Girl" is singular; "girls" is plural.* —*n.* **1.** The singular number in grammar. **2.** A word in the singular number.

- **skylight** /skī′ līt′/ *n.* Window in a roof or ceiling.
- **slogan** /slō′ gən/ *n.* **1.** Word or phrase used like a war cry by a group; motto: *"Safety First" is our slogan.* **2.** A battle cry.
- **snorkel** /snôr′ kəl/ *n.* **1.** Shaft for taking in air and letting out gases, which allows submarines to remain under water for long periods of time. **2.** A curved tube which enables swimmers to breathe under water while swimming near the surface.
- **soapsuds** /sōp′ sudz′/ *n. pl.* Bubbles and foam made with soap and water.
- **sodium** /sō′ dē əm/ *n.* A silver-white chemical element occurring in nature only in combination with other elements: *Sodium is found in salt and soda.*
- **softball** /sôft′ bôl′/ *n.* **1.** A kind of baseball game, played with a larger ball and lighter bats than baseball. **2.** Ball used in this game.
- **solar** /sō′ lər/ *adj.* **1.** Having to do with the sun: *a solar eclipse.* **2.** Determined by the sun: *solar time.*
- **sparkle** /spär′ kəl/ *v.* **1.** Send out little sparks; shine; glitter. **2.** Be brilliant; be lively: *Her conversation sparkles with humor.* —*n.* A little spark; glitter.
- **spectacle** /spek′ tə kəl/ *n.* **1.** Thing to look at; sight: *A quarrel is an unpleasant spectacle.* **2.** A public show or display: *The army parade was a fine spectacle.*
- **spectator** /spek′ tā tər/ *n.* Person who looks on without taking part: *the spectators at the football game.*
- **spicy** /spī′ sē/ *adj.* **1.** Flavored with spice: *The cookies were rich and spicy.* **2.** Like spice: *The apples had a spicy taste.* **3.** Lively; keen: *spicy conversation; spicy gossip.* **spicier, spiciest.**
- **spinal** /spī′ nəl/ *adj.* Of the spine or backbone: *a spinal injury.*
- **spiral** /spī′ rəl/ *n.* A winding and gradually widening coil: *A watch spring is a spiral.* —*adj.* Coiled: *a spiral staircase.* —*v.* Move in a spiral: *The flaming airplane spiraled to earth.*
- **splendor** /splen′ dər/ *n.* **1.** Great brightness; brilliant light: *the splendor of the rising sun.* **2.** Magnificent show; glory: *the splendor of the king's coronation.*
- **sponsor** /spon′ sər/ *n.* Person who is responsible for a person or thing. —*v.* Act as sponsor for: *Some stores sponsor television programs as a means of advertising what they sell.*
- **squabble** /skwob′ əl/ *n.* A petty, noisy quarrel: *Children's squabbles annoy their parents.* —*v.* Take part in a petty, noisy quarrel. **squabbled, squabbling.**
- **squander** /skwon′ dər/ *v.* Spend foolishly; waste: *He squandered his time and money in gambling.*
- **squirrel** /skwėr′ əl/ *n.* **1.** Small, bushy-tailed animal that usually lives in trees and eats nuts. **2.** Its gray, reddish, or dark-brown fur.
- **stadium** /stā′ dē əm/ *n.* Place shaped like an oval or a U, consisting of tiers of seats around an open field. *pl.* **stadiums** or **stadia** /stā′ dē ə/.
- **stampede** /stam pēd′/ *n.* **1.** A sudden scattering or headlong flight of a frightened herd of cattle or horses. **2.** Any headlong flight of a large group. —*v.* **1.** Scatter or flee in a stampede. **2.** Cause to stampede. **stampeded, stampeding.**
- **standard** /stan′ dərd/ *n.* **1.** Anything taken as a basis of comparison; model. **2.** Flag; emblem: *The dragon was the standard of China.* —*adj.* **1.** According to rule: *standard spelling.* **2.** Having recognized authority: *Scott is a standard author.*
- **stencil** /sten′ səl/ *n.* **1.** A thin sheet of metal, paper, etc., having letters or designs cut through it. When it is laid on a surface and ink or colors are spread on, the designs are made on the surface. **2.** Letters or designs so made. —*v.* Mark or paint with a stencil.
- **sterile** /ster′ əl/ *adj.* **1.** Free from living germs: *a doctor's sterile instruments.* **2.** Barren; not fertile: *Sterile land does not produce good crops.*
- **stubborn** /stub′ ərn/ *adj.* **1.** Fixed in purpose or opinion; not giving in to the argument or requests. **2.** Hard to deal with: *I had a stubborn cough.*

/a/ ran /ā/ rain /ã/ care /ä/ car /e/ hen /ē/ he /ėr/ her /i/ in /ī/ ice /o/ not /ō/ no /ô/ off /u/ us /ū/ use /ü/ tool /u̇/ took /ou/ cow /oi/ boy /ch/ church /hw/ when /ng/ sing /sh/ ship /ᴛʜ/ this /th/ thin /zh/ vision /ə/ about, taken, pencil, lemon, circus

- **studio** /stü' dē ō/ *or* /stū' dē ō/ *n.* **1.** Workroom of a painter, sculptor, photographer, or other artist. **2.** Place where motion pictures are made. **3.** Place from which a radio or television program is broadcast. *pl.* **studios.**
- **stupor** /stü' pər/ *or* /stū' pər/ *n.* A dazed condition; loss or lessening of the power to feel: *The injured man lay in a stupor, unable to speak.*
- **succor** /suk' ər/ *n.* Aid; help: *The nurse gave succor to the wounded soldiers.* —*v.* Give help to.
- **suet** /sü' ət/ *n.* The hard fat of cattle or sheep, used in cooking and for making tallow.
- **suitable** /süt' ə bəl/ *or* /sūt' ə bəl/ *adj.* Fitting; proper.
- **suitor** /sü' tər/ *n.* A man who is courting a woman: *The princess had many suitors.*
- **sunrise** /sun' rīz'/ *n.* The coming up of the sun; first appearance of the sun in the morning.
- **surface** /sėr' fəs/ *n.* **1.** The outside of anything: *An egg has a smooth surface.* **2.** Any face or side of a thing: *A cube has six surfaces.* **3.** Outward appearance. —*v.* **1.** Make smooth; cover smoothly: *surface a road.* **2.** Rise to the surface of the water. **surfaced, surfacing.**
- **sympathy** /sim' pə thē/ *n.* **1.** Sharing another's sorrows or trouble: *sympathy for a person who is ill.* **2.** Having the same feeling: *The sympathy between the twins was so great that they often laughed or cried at the same time.* **3.** Agreement; favor: *She is in sympathy with my plan.* *pl.* **sympathies.**

t

- **tailor** /tā' lər/ *n.* Person whose business it is to make, repair, or alter clothes. —*v.* Make by tailor's work: *a well-tailored suit.*
- **tailspin** /tāl' spin'/ *n.* Downward movement of an airplane with the nose first and the tail spinning in a circle above.
- **tally** /tal' ē/ *n.* **1.** Stick of wood in which notches are cut to represent numbers, formerly used to show the amount of a debt or payment. **2.** Anything on which a score is kept. **3.** Account; score. **4.** Mark made for a certain number; notch. *pl.* **tallies.** —*v.* **1.** Mark on a tally; count up. **2.** Agree with: *Your account tallies with mine.* **tallied, tallying.**
- **tassel** /tas' əl/ *n.* **1.** A hanging bunch of threads, fastened together at one end. **2.** Something like a hanging bunch of threads: *corn tassels.* —*v.* Grow tassels: *Corn tassels just before ears form.*
- **tenant** /ten' ənt/ *n.* **1.** Person paying rent for the use of another person's land or building. **2.** Person or thing that occupies: *Birds are tenants of the trees.* —*v.* Inhabit; occupy as a tenant: *That house is not tenanted.*
- **tendril** /ten' drəl/ *n.* **1.** A threadlike part of a climbing plant that attaches itself to something and helps support the plant. **2.** Something similar in appearance to the tendril of a plant: *curly tendrils of hair.*
- **tenor** /ten' ər/ *n.* **1.** The highest adult male voice: *Bass and tenor are two parts for men's voices.* **2.** Singer with such a voice. **3.** Part sung by such a voice.
- **termite** /tėr' mīt/ *n.* Insect, sometimes called the white ant, that eats the wood of buildings, furniture, and other material containing cellulose.
- **terrible** /ter' ə bəl/ *adj.* Causing great fear; dreadful; awful.
- **terror** /ter' ər/ *n.* **1.** Great fear: *a terror of thunder.* **2.** Cause of great fear.
- **testify** /tes' tə fī/ *v.* Give evidence; bear witness; declare. **testified, testifying.**
- **textile** /teks' təl/ *adj.* **1.** Woven: *Cloth is a textile fabric.* **2.** Suitable for weaving: *textile materials.* **3.** Having something to do with weaving: *the textile industry.* —*n.* **1.** Woven fabric; cloth: *Beautiful textiles are sold in Paris.* **2.** Material that can be woven.
- **theory** /thē' ər ē/ *n.* **1.** Explanation based on thought or on observation and reasoning. **2.** Principles or methods of a science or art rather than its practice: *the theory of music.* **3.** Idea or opinion about something: *My theory is that the fire was started by a careless smoker.* *pl.* **theories.**
- **throughout** /thrü' out'/ *prep.* All the way through; through all; in every part of. —*adv.* In every part.
- **tidal** /tī' dəl/ *adj.* Of tides; having tides; caused by tides: *a tidal river; a tidal wave.*
- **timid** /tim' id/ *adj.* Easily frightened; shy: *Deer are timid animals; a timid child.*
- **tinsel** /tin' səl/ *n.* **1.** Glittering strips or threads made of thin copper, brass, or some other metal, and used to trim Christmas trees. **2.** Anything showy but having little value.

- **tiptoe** /tip′ tō′/ *n.* The tips of the toes. *–v.* Walk on the tips of the toes.
- **tonsil** /ton′ səl/ *n.* Either of the two small, oval masses of tissue on the sides of the throat, just back of the mouth.
- **toothache** /tüth′ āk′/ *n.* Pain in the tooth.
- **torture** /tôr′ chər/ *n.* **1.** Act of inflicting very severe pain. **2.** Very severe pain. *–v.* Cause very severe pain to. **tortured, torturing.**
- **total** /tō′ təl/ *n.* The whole amount: *His expenses reached a total of $100.* *–v.* **1.** Reach an amount of: *The expenses total $100.* **2.** Add; find the sum of: *total a column of figures.* *–adj.* **1.** Whole: *the total cost.* **2.** Complete: *total darkness.*
- **touchdown** /tuch′ doun′/ *n.* **1.** Score made in putting the football to the ground behind the opponent's goal line. **2.** Act of landing an airplane.
- **towboat** /tō′ bōt′/ *n.* Tugboat, especially one with a flat bottom, used on a river.
- **towel** /tou′ əl/ *n.* Piece of cloth or paper for wiping and drying something wet.
- **tractor** /trak′ tər/ *n.* Engine which moves on wheels or on two endless tracks, used for pulling wagons, trucks, plows, or other vehicles.
- **tranquil** /tran′ kwəl/ *adj.* Calm; peaceful, quiet: *a tranquil morning; a tranquil scene; a tranquil spirit.*
- **transistor** /tran zis′ tər/ *n.* A very small crystal device that amplifies electricity by controlling the flow of electrons. Transistors have replaced tubes in many small radios.
- **travel** /trav′ əl/ *v.* **1.** Go from one place to another. **2.** Move; proceed; pass: *Sound travels in waves.* *–n.* Going from one place to another.
- **treadle** /tred′ əl/ *n.* Lever or pedal worked by the foot to impart motion to a machine: *the treadle of a sewing machine.*
- **tremor** /trem′ ər/ *n.* **1.** A shaking or trembling: *nervous tremor.* **2.** Thrill of excitement.
- **trespass** /tres′ pəs/ *v.* **1.** Go on somebody's property without any right. **2.** Go beyond the limits of what is right, proper, or polite. **3.** Do wrong; sin. *–n.* **1.** Wrong; sin: *"Forgive us our trespasses as we forgive those who trespass against us."* **2.** Going on somebody's property without any right. **3.** Going beyond the limits of what is right. *pl.* **trespasses.**
- **trial** /trī′ əl/ *n.* **1.** Test; process of trying or testing. **2.** The process of examining and deciding a case in court. **3.** Trouble; hardship. *–adj.* For a test: *a trial trip.* **on trial, 1.** Being tried. **2.** For a test.
- **tribal** /trī′ bəl/ *adj.* Having to do with a tribe; of a tribe: *tribal customs.*
- **triumph** /trī′ umf/ *n.* **1.** Victory; success: *triumph over the enemy.* **2.** Joy because of victory: *shouts of triumph.* *–v.* **1.** Gain a victory: *Our team triumphed over theirs.* **2.** Rejoice because of victory or success.
- **trivial** /triv′ ē əl/ *adj.* Not important: *a trivial matter.*
- **trolley** /trol′ ē/ *n.* **1.** Pulley at the end of a pole which moves against a wire to carry electricity to a streetcar or an electric engine. **2.** Pulley running on an overhead track, used to support and move a load. **3.** A trolley car; a trolley bus. *pl.* **trolleys.**
- **tropical** /trop′ ik əl/ *adj.* Having to do with the tropics: *Bananas are a tropical fruit.*
- **trowel** /trou′ əl/ *n.* **1.** Tool with a broad, flat blade for spreading or smoothing plaster or mortar. **2.** Tool with a curved blade for taking up plants and loosening dirt.
- **truant** /trü′ ənt/ *n.* **1.** A child who stays away from school without permission. **2.** Person who neglects duty. *–adj.* Neglecting duty.
- **tumor** /tü′ mər/ *or* /tū′ mər/ *n.* An abnormal or diseased swelling in any part of the body.
- **tunnel** /tun′ əl/ *n.* An underground passage: *The railroad tunnel passes through the mountain.* *–v.* Make a tunnel: *The workers tunneled under the river.*
- **turkey** /tėr′ kē/ *n.* **1.** A large North American bird used for food. **2.** Flesh of the turkey, used for food. *pl.* **turkeys.**
- **turmoil** /tėr′ moil/ *n.* Commotion; tumult; disturbance: *Six robberies in one night left the village in a turmoil.*
- **tutor** /tū′ tər/ *or* /tü′ tər/ *n.* A private teacher: *Those children have tutors instead of going to school.* *–v.* Teach; instruct: *She was tutored at home during her illness.*
- **tyrant** /tī′ rənt/ *n.* **1.** Person who uses power cruelly or unjustly. **2.** A cruel or unjust ruler.

/a/ ran /ā/ rain /ã/ care /ä/ car /e/ hen /ē/ he /ėr/ her /i/ in /ī/ ice /o/ not /ō/ no /ô/ off
/u/ us /ū/ use /ü/ tool /u̇/ took /ou/ cow /oi/ boy /ch/ church /hw/ when /ng/ sing /sh/ ship
/ᴛʜ/ this /th/ thin /zh/ vision /ə/ about, taken, pencil, lemon, circus

u

- **umpire** /um′ pīr/ *n.* **1.** Person who rules on the plays in a game. **2.** Person chosen to settle a dispute. *–v.* Act as umpire in (a game or dispute). **umpired, umpiring.**
- **uproar** /up′ rôr′/ *n.* **1.** A noisy disturbance: *an uproar in town when the lion escaped from the circus.* **2.** A loud or confused noise.

v

- **vacuum** /vak′ ū əm/ *n.* **1.** An empty space without even air in it. **2.** An enclosed space from which almost all air or gas has been removed. **3.** A void: *Her mother's death left a vacuum in her life. pl.* **vacuums, vacua** /vak′ ū ə/. *–v.* Clean with a vacuum cleaner: *He vacuumed the rug carefully.*
- **valley** /val′ ē/ *n.* **1.** Low lands between hills. **2.** Region drained by a river.
- **valor** /val′ ər/ *n.* Bravery; courage.
- **value** /val′ ū/ *n.* **1.** The real worth. **2.** High worth; excellence; usefulness. **3.** Power to buy: *the value of the dollar.* **4.** Estimated worth: *She placed a value on her furniture.* *–v.* **1.** Estimate the value of. **2.** Regard highly. **valued, valuing.**
- **vandal** /van′ dəl/ *n.* Person who destroys beautiful or valuable things on purpose. [*Vandal* is derived from the name *Vandals,* a barbarian people who invaded parts of Europe and Africa, and in A.D. 455 plundered Rome.]
- **vapor** /vā′ pər/ *n.* **1.** Steam from boiling water; fog; mist: *The vapor of the morning mist rose along the river.* **2.** Gas formed from a substance that is usually a liquid or a solid: *gasoline vapor.*
- **vassal** /vas′ əl/ *n.* Person who held land from a lord or superior, to whom in return he gave help in war or some other service. *–adj.* Subordinate; like a vassal: *a vassal nation.*
- **venture** /ven′ chər/ *n.* A risky undertaking: *Her courage is equal to any venture.* *–v.* **1.** Expose to risk or danger: *Men venture their lives in war.* **2.** Dare: *venture to go near the edge.* **3.** Dare to say: *venture a protest.* **ventured, venturing.**
- **verbal** /vėr′ bəl/ *adj.* **1.** Having to do with words; in words: *A description is a verbal picture.* **2.** Oral; expressed in spoken words: *a verbal promise.*
- **vessel** /ves′ əl/ *n.* **1.** Large boat; ship: *Ocean liners and other vessels are usually docked by tugboats.* **2.** A hollow container or holder like a cup, bowl, pitcher, bottle, barrel, or the like. **3.** Tube carrying blood or other fluid: *Veins and arteries are blood vessels.*
- **vibrate** /vī′ brāt/ *v.* **1.** Move rapidly to and fro. **2.** Quiver; be moved. **vibrated, vibrating.**
- **vicar** /vik′ ər/ *n.* **1.** Clergyman in charge of one chapel in a parish. **2.** Person acting in place of another.
- **victor** /vik′ tər/ *n.* Winner; conqueror: *a victor in the tennis match.*
- **viewpoint** /vū′ point′/ *n.* Attitude of mind: *A heavy rain that is good from the viewpoint of farmers may be bad from the viewpoint of tourists.*
- **vigil** /vij′ əl/ *n.* **1.** Act of watching; watch; a watch during the usual hours for sleep: *a father's vigil over his sick child.* **2.** The day and night before a solemn religious festival.
- **vigor** /vig′ ər/ *n.* **1.** Active strength or force: *He argued his point with vigor.* **2.** Healthy energy: *The vigor of the old man's mind decreased.*
- **villain** /vil′ ən/ *n.* **1.** Wicked person. **2.** Playful name for a mischievous person.
- **visor** /vī′ zər/ *n.* **1.** The movable front part of a helmet, covering the face. **2.** The part of a brim of a hat that sticks out in front. **3.** A shield that can be lowered from above to the inside of a car windshield to shield the eyes from the sun.
- **visual** /vizh′ ü əl/ *adj.* **1.** Having something to do with sight: *Being near-sighted is a visual problem.* **2.** Visible; able to be seen.
- **vital** /vī′ təl/ *adj.* **1.** Of life: *Growth and decay are vital forces.* **2.** Necessary to life: *The heart is a vital organ.* **3.** Essential; very necessary: *Education of the young is vital to the future of our country.*
- **vocal** /vō′ kəl/ *adj.* **1.** Having to do with voice or speaking: *The tongue is a vocal organ.* **2.** Made with the voice: *vocal music.* **3.** Having a voice; giving forth sound. **4.** Inclined to talk freely: *She became vocal with anger.*
- **volley** /vol′ ē/ *n.* **1.** A shower of stones, bullets, or other missiles: *A volley of arrows came down upon the knights.* **2.** A noisy burst of many things at once. **3.** Discharge of many guns at once. *pl.* **volleys.** *–v.* Discharge or be discharged in a volley: *Cannon volleyed on all sides.*

- **vowel** /vou′ əl/ *n.* **1.** An open sound produced by the voice, such as the sound in *broad* that is spelled with the letters *oa.* **2.** The letters that stand for such a sound. *a, e, i, o,* and *u* are vowels. —*adj.* Having to do with a vowel; of a vowel: *a vowel sound; a vowel letter.*
- **voyage** /voi′ ij/ *n.* **1.** A journey or travel by water; cruise. **2.** A journey or travel through the air or through space. —*v.* Make or take a voyage.
- **vulgar** /vul′ gər/ *adj.* **1.** Coarse; not refined; showing lack of good breeding, manners, or taste: *vulgar words.* **2.** Having to do with the common people: *The vulgar language differs from the language used by lawyers or doctors.*

w

- **waddle** /wod′ əl/ *v.* Walk with short steps and an awkward, swaying motion, as a duck does. **waddled, waddling.** —*n.* Act of waddling: *a duck's waddle.*
- **wardrobe** /wôrd′ rōb′/ *n.* **1.** Stock of clothes: *shopping for a spring wardrobe.* **2.** Room, closet, or piece of furniture for holding clothes.
- **warfare** /wär′ fãr′/ *n.* War; fighting.
- **wealthy** /wel′ thē/ *adj.* Having wealth; rich. **wealthier, wealthiest.**
- **weasel** /wē′ zəl/ *n.* A quick, small, sly animal with a slender body and short legs, eating rats, mice, birds, and eggs.
- **weevil** /wē′ vəl/ *n.* Small beetle whose larvae eat grain, nuts, fruits, or the stems of the leaves of cotton plants and other plants.
- **whinny** /hwin′ ē/ *n.* The sound a horse makes. *pl.* **whinnies.** —*v.* Make such a sound. **whinnied, whinnying.**
- **whitewash** /hwīt′ wosh′/ *n.* Liquid for whitening walls, woodwork, or other surfaces: *Whitewash is usually made of lime and water.* —*v.* **1.** Whiten with whitewash. **2.** Cover the faults or mistakes of. **3.** Defeat in a game without a score for the loser.
- **wiener** /wē′ nər/ *n.* Frankfurter. [*Wiener* is shortened from the German phrase *Wiener Würstchen,* meaning "sausage of Vienna (capital of Austria)."]
- **witchcraft** /wich′ kraft′/ *n.* What a witch does or is supposed to be able to do; magic power.
- **wither** /wiᴛʜ′ ər/ *v.* **1.** Make or become dry and lifeless; dry up; shrivel; fade: *The sun withered the grass.* **2.** Cause to feel ashamed or confused: *She withered the girl with a look.*
- **withhold** /with′ hōld′/ *or* /wiᴛʜ′ hōld′/ *v.* **1.** Refuse to give: *withhold consent.* **2.** Hold back; keep back: *The general withheld two regiments from the attack.* **withheld, withholding.**
- **worry** /wėr′ ē/ *n.* Care; anxiety; trouble. *pl.* **worries.** —*v.* **1.** Feel anxious. **2.** Make anxious; trouble. **3.** Annoy. **4.** Shake with the teeth; bite at: *The dog worried the rat.* **worried, worrying.**
- **worthwhile** /wėrth′ hwīl′/ *adj.* Worth time, attention, or trouble; having merit.

y

- **yodel** /yō′ dəl/ *v.* Sing with frequent changes from the ordinary voice to a forced, shrill voice and back again. —*n.* Act or sound of yodeling.

4 5 6 7 8 9 10 VHVH 84 83 82 81 80 79 78 77 76

Dicky Padhiar